My Children's Children

Raising Young Citizens
in the Age of Columbine

Robert A. Saul, MD

FOR

Bradley and Ben

DEDICATED TO

The victims and the families of the Columbine High School and
Sandy Hook Elementary School shootings

Author's notes

The events of April 20, 1999 at Columbine High School in Littleton, CO have had a permanent influence on me. Previously engaged in numerous community improvement events, I was suddenly stunned when I considered what I could do to prevent such actions in my community of Greenwood, SC. How could I possibly make a difference? To honor the fallen, community improvement efforts needed to be re-doubled. And yet that still didn't seem enough. Advancing an agenda to promote citizenship was the logical additional component that was needed.

This book represents such an effort—to combine efforts at community improvement and citizenship. Chapter 2 discusses my journey through the process of self-discovery and advocacy. I quote health-care futurist Leland Kaiser who reminds us that for anything that happens in our community, we need to remember, "I am the problem, I am the solution, I am the resource." As I reviewed the over 160 articles that I wrote as op-ed pieces for the local newspaper since 1999, I realized that I had the rare opportunity to use my role as a pediatrician to help drive these efforts. I have no pretense that my words are the "gospel" for these endeavors. They are intended to provide some guidance based on my years of experience and to generate discussion that gets people working together for a common purpose.

I emphasize in the second section of the book about learning to be the best parent you can be. Parenting is critical to the discussions in this book, but parenting itself is insufficient. In the Five Steps paradigm that I present, the other steps–get involved, stay involved, love for others, and forgiveness—are important and deserve equal attention. Over the course of the book, I attempt to highlight the importance of raising good citizens who will engage in the activities of caring for each other and improving their community. These activities should be the goals of parenting.

Ten years after the Columbine shooting, my family visited the Columbine Memorial (www.columbinememorial.org) in 2009. The cover photograph of me was taken at that time. Walking around the memorial and reading the stories about the victims on the Ring of Remembrance and the comments etched in stone on the Wall of Healing was an incredibly moving experience. It provided even greater impetus for me to try and tell my message beyond the confines of the local newspaper and colleagues around the country.

As I was finishing the manuscript in late 2012, another mass shooting at a school occurred. The massacre at Sandy Hook in Newtown, CT was another grim reminder of the inability of our society to protect its most vulnerable citizens. More guns are not the answer. Our society already has more guns than other civilized societies and we are clearly not safer. More civility and more responsibility for taking care of others is what we need. President Obama's poignant remarks at the Sandy Hook memorial service provide the logical conclusion to the book.

I would like to dedicate the book to the victims and the families of the Columbine High School and Sandy Hook Elementary School shootings. The strength of the families and their ability to carry on in the midst of such horrific events gives me greater purpose to honor their mission. I hope this book and its messages inspire parents, young and old, to raise their children to be good citizens for themselves, their families, and their fellow citizens.

Bob Saul
October 6, 2013

Advance Praise for
My Children's Children

"*Bob Saul began his pediatric training with us at Duke and from those initial years onward has unceasingly demonstrated his lifelong passion for children and their families. The principles of the Five Steps to Community Improvement exemplify his commitment to exploit the experiences of his life and pediatric career to advocate tangible ways for parents to raise their children with the goal of outstanding citizenship. MY CHILDREN'S CHILDREN provides a unique and hopefully lasting approach to both parenting and community involvement.*"

Samuel L. Katz, M.D., D.Sc.(hon.), Wilburt Cornell Davison
Professor & Chairman emeritus, Department of Pediatrics,
Duke University School of Medicine.

"*MY CHILDREN'S CHILDREN demonstrates Dr. Saul's commitment to improving the health of all children, especially those at high risk for various problems. I am impressed by his commitment to make a real difference in the lives of children and the communities of South Carolina and beyond. He recognizes the multiple factors that contribute to the health and well being of children and their families. This book makes substantial contributions toward promoting an holistic approach to childhood education and should have a lasting impact in future community improvement efforts. It gives us a clear road map for raising good citizens—a great need in our country today.*"

Richard Riley, former Governor of South Carolina and
the former US Secretary of Education

"Dr. Saul is a deeply committed member of the American Academy of Pediatrics, which represents 60,000 pediatricians dedicated to the health, safety and well being of infants, children, adolescents and young adults. His book presents his perspective toward raising children to be productive citizens who make significant contributions to their communities. MY CHILDREN'S CHILDREN reflects his work and thinking over his career and especially the last 15 years. This helpful book serves to remind parents and children's professionals alike that the work of caring for children and the work of improving communities requires the continuing and collaborative work of many. This book will serve our children and families well."

James Perrin, MD, Professor of Pediatrics at Harvard Medical School and former director of the Division of General Pediatrics at the MassGeneral Hospital for Children.

Table of Contents

Columbine was a momentous event in the history of the country...Even in the midst of tragedy we've seen the best, the best there is to see about our nation and about human nature.

(President Clinton, Columbine Memorial groundbreaking, 2007; inscription from the wall of the Columbine Memorial)

Section 1
INTRODUCTION

Chapter 1

Raising Young Citizens in the Age of Columbine

Since 1999, I have written a series of articles for the *Index-Journal* in Greenwood, South Carolina. These articles, more than 165 in number, have addressed timely issues of local and national concern. I organized these articles into five categories or what I call the Five Steps to Community Improvement. These five steps constitute a paradigm that considers all of the systems that have to work together in order to bring about positive changes in our families and in our communities. Upon the urging of colleagues, friends, and readers, I have decided to revise and compile these articles into a single volume that focuses on how we can foster good citizenship in the broadest sense of that term.

The Five Steps to Community Improvement

The five steps are: 1) learn to be the best parent you can be, 2) get involved, 3) stay involved, 4) love for others and 5) forgiveness. These steps emphasize the individual importance of certain words and deeds and at the same time emphasize the inter-relatedness of all our words and deeds. The words "five steps to community improvement" were carefully chosen. I firmly believe that words and deeds that follow these five steps will logically lead to community improvement. Individual improvements in our children and citizens will lead to community gains, and community improvements will provide an enriched environment for all of our children. The effect of these interactions is not simply additive. The effect is synergistic (or interactive) and usually much greater than the sums of individual efforts. This synergy is one reason why community improvement efforts are dynamic and exciting.

I have to make a confession. Over the course of the last thirteen years, I have shared my thoughts in the form of op-ed articles with colleagues and friends all over the country. As the audience expanded, I was pleased to spread the message and receive input from multiple sources. However, I soon discovered that the real audience was me. Yes, I found that these articles and their action steps were not abstract concepts that I was relating to other people. As I wrote the articles and considered their significance, the issues addressed have become personal to-do items. I realized that if I really wanted to make a difference I had better practice what I preach by becoming a more effective husband, father, physician, communicator, facilitator, and even author. Since I want to improve in all of these roles daily, I need to match the deeds with my words.

Over the last several years, I also realized that my suggestions are well suited for new parents (and really any parents) as a guide to how to raise children. But I specifically did not want to write what I considered to be a standard guide for raising children primarily because of my discomfort with setting myself up as a parenting expert. I have a lot of experience but I certainly do not profess to have all of the answers for raising children. Instead, this book presents a broad framework for how to raise a good citizen. These two concepts (raising children and future citizens) are vitally linked. Solidly nurtured children become good citizens at the same time that they become healthy adults, both socially and spiritually. I approach this book from the citizenship side because the only way our society can continue to improve is for all of us to have a common purpose—to care for, to love, to nurture, to empathize with, to support, and to come to the aid of others. I want my children, the children that I have cared for as a physician, and all of the children on whom I might have a positive influence to strive for that goal in their lives. This starts in our homes and then spreads to our community. If we learn to be the best parents we can be, get involved, stay involved, love others, and exercise forgiveness, we will make significant strides toward cultivating good citizens.

One question arising from my argument might be this: "The Five Steps concept is nice, but why does it matter, especially when parents already have enough responsibilities raising their young children?" The answer is simple—this concept is absolutely critical. By the end of the book, I hope that the truth of this is obvious. If we don't raise our children to understand the essential interplay of everything in our lives and to understand that everything we do has an impact on others, we have failed. In the parenting chapter, I will discuss evidence that emphasizes the critical period of early childhood development (0-3 years) and its effect on health.

I am using health in a broad sense, meaning physical health, mental health, educational health, financial health, and social health. I mean the interplay of all these factors. They are all critical to the health of our children and the health of our society. Unhealthy children cannot contribute to a healthy society, and an unhealthy society is severely impaired in its ability to raise healthy children. I do not refer to children with special health care needs as unhealthy. However, the way their needs are addressed can be healthful or not. Like all children, special needs children provide immeasurable benefits and joy to their families and communities.

Citizenship

Citizen is defined as "a member of a state or nation who owes allegiance to its government and is entitled to its protection." On a local level, the definition can be "an inhabitant of a city or town, especially one entitled to its privileges and franchises." The first definition notes an extremely important point regarding citizenship—citizenship's entitlements requires active involvement in its activities. Allegiance means loyalty to the principles of the government. The ultimate purpose of mandatory public education is to prepare our young men and women for a mature life in the role of citizen.

If our young men and women are to be good citizens, they need to learn basic principles of civic engagement and community improvement.

The basic principles of citizenship should be used along with the paradigm of the Five Steps To Community Improvement as a core level of interaction between children, families and society. Why?

- Health care futurist Leland Kaiser rightfully notes that for community improvement to occur each citizen must take personal responsibility for the activities in their community. These activities might already be positive ones or, more than likely, might be areas open to significant improvement. "For anything that happens in our community," says Leland Kaiser as he challenges each of us as individuals and our society as a whole, "I am the problem, I am the solution, I am the resource." Those are pretty simple words but the message is a powerful one. We have to respond by saying "I have to take personal ownership for the issues in my community (I am the problem), I have to work with my fellow citizens (I am the solution), and I need to be willing to devote my continuing energies to the community (I am the resource)." We could just as easily substitute the "I" for "we" in the sentence—We are the problem, we are the solution, we are the resource. Only by active engagement can we truly make a difference.
- The Five Steps provide a paradigm for ways to engage in the active participation needed for students to make the transition to adult citizens in society (further explained in Chapter 2).

Why a Pediatrician Is Talking about Citizenship

As a pediatrician, I have a tremendous responsibility to children and their families. Parents seek medical care and trusted counsel from a respected health care provider with the essential abilities—to listen, to diagnose, to provide care, to empathize, to prescribe, to recommend and to treat their patients like one of their own. While pediatricians do not use holy water in their interactions, they do invest an incredible amount of professional experience and emotional energy as they engage in partnerships with the families they serve.

I have always marveled at how my pediatric colleagues refer to their patients as "my children." Initially, I found that to be a bit presumptuous. Families bring their children to the pediatrician for medical care, not to cede control of them to the doctor. But now I understand how they feel. Physicians actively engaged in the medical care of their pediatric patients invest their physical, mental, and emotional energy in the care of these children. Their patients effectively do become "their children." Years later when these children grow up and have their own children, pediatricians have the true privilege of seeing and, perhaps, caring for this next generation. The pride in this continuing relationship can be as palpable as the pride that pediatricians who are grandparents have in their own grandchildren.

It is in this spirit that "My Children's Children" is written—to provide a legacy of thoughts and suggestions that could potentially have a positive and lasting impact on my children and their children, my grandchildren. What do I mean by my children and their children? First and foremost, I mean my own two sons and their possible future progeny. Second—and equally important—I mean the children that I have cared for in twenty-four years of primary care pediatrics and, now, their children. And, finally, I mean all the children that I can possibly affect as a staunch child advocate in my community and beyond. I hope to positively influence these three groups to fulfill my nurturing role as a father, as a physician and as a fellow citizen.

A Tribute to my Mother

My mother was a remarkable woman. She was extremely dedicated to her two sons. My parents divorced when I was 9 years old. While we were a family of means based on the wealth of my mother's parents, my mother had no substantive emotional support from her family and had to deal with issues of spousal alcoholism and my father's propensity to verbal and physical abuse by herself. Her ability to strike out on her own and to empathize with, care for, and genuinely love virtually everyone she met was indeed remarkable. I realize now that the values I have formulated are those of my mother.

My mother was always engaged in the community and genuinely cared for her fellow citizens and for the life of the community. My mother wrote a journal (excerpted in Chapter 2) during the turbulent 1960s with the Vietnam War and the assassination of Martin Luther King, Jr. as the backdrop. She was called to action from the events of the day.

The events at Columbine High School in Littleton, CO were a similar call to action for me. Since 1999, I have been on this Five Steps journey, suggesting ways to raise young citizens in the years after Columbine. Events and powers beyond my control have beckoned me to act on behalf of others. I welcome the challenge.

This book is for parents who like my mother want to raise their children the right way—to be good parents and good citizens. Healthy children (physically, mentally, educationally, financially and socially) are good citizens. Healthy children are our future. Let the Five Steps be a guide. Oh—and, thank you, Mom.

Chapter 2

Littleton, Colorado and Five Steps

Letter to the editor, *Index-Journal* (Greenwood, SC) [published May 5, 1999]

After the tragedy at Columbine High School on April 20, 1999, I felt compelled to write a letter to the editor of my local paper in South Carolina, the Index-Journal. Little did I know the journey this would begin. An excerpt follows:

> Last night I watched a town meeting in New Jersey attended by Vice President Gore, Governor Whitman, Secretary of Education Riley, the District Attorney from Jefferson County, Colorado and numerous other dignitaries, parents and students. It was entitled "Lessons from Littleton." As I watched, I tried to understand my own emotions following the devastating events of April 20, 1999 at Columbine High School in Littleton, Colorado. I went to school in Colorado, and my mother lives in Littleton. Yet it is not that attachment that has had such a profound impact on me. I <u>personally</u> have felt this tragedy. This is not just a tragedy in Littleton but one in every community in the United States—yes, even Greenwood, South Carolina. We have fostered a climate of moral decay in the United States that was sadly dramatized last week in Littleton. We all need to take some personal responsibility for this. Lack of responsibility and lack of accountability in daily personal and interpersonal lives have contributed to the inevitable growth of intolerance, hatred, violence and drugs in today's

society. We all need to ask ourselves the question—How can I be sure that this doesn't happen in Greenwood, South Carolina?

Let's be honest. We cannot eliminate all the acts of severely mentally ill individuals, and the tragedy in Littleton was obviously performed by two very disturbed people. But we can change the way people feel about themselves and others! We can also change the availability of the weapons of death and the graphic depiction of gratuitous violence. We could devote a whole section of the *Index-Journal* to these latter issues, but I wanted to address the issues of relationships.

One last note. Some of the most striking scenes I have ever watched on TV in my lifetime have been the interviews with families touched by the tragedy in Littleton—families that have lost sons, daughters, sisters, brothers and a father. Their faith in God and their ability to cope with such devastation have reminded me again about the importance of spirituality in everything we do. Let us all learn from the "lessons from Littleton."

Shortly thereafter, I realized that I had set forth a blueprint of action for myself—that I needed to try to articulate ideas worthy of consideration for community action and improvement. I knew that my role was to be a facilitator and to sound a call to action.

Five Steps, 2005

I was on my way with only a very rudimentary blueprint to follow, but I knew that I had a purpose and wanted to fulfill it. Multiple newspaper articles followed the first. I found myself also wanting to share this journey with fellow medical professionals. They have a significant responsibility to improve their communities by not only improving the medical health (physical and mental) of their patients but in tending to the social health of their patients. My call to action was published in the *Journal of the South Carolina Medical Association* (Vol. 101, Feb. 2005, pages 35-37) under the title "Columbine High School—April 20, 1999. What Can I Do?" [Minor edits for clarity]

The day, April 20th, 1999 started innocently enough. I was in Chicago for a strategic planning session of the Executive Committee of the Section on Genetics and Birth Defects for the American Academy of Pediatrics. We spent all day in front of flip charts trying to plan a future direction for the section. This exercise was reasonably satisfying, but I was tired and ready to get home to my family.

I caught a shuttle to the airport late afternoon and went to the gate to await my flights home to South Carolina. "I'll just relax and read my book," I thought to myself. But there was quite a hubbub near the TV monitors in the gate area. A shooting at a high school, Columbine High School, in Littleton, Colorado? How could that be? Unfortunately in my lifetime, murderous rampages have been all too common. Wait a minute – the shooters were fellow high school students! And they murdered some of their fellow students in cold blood!

As the story unfolded over the days to follow, I was numb. I followed all the news to try and understand how this could happen. I felt powerless. The incident was in Colorado and I was in South Carolina. (I graduated from high school, college, and medical school in Colorado so I had more than a passing interest in Colorado affairs). I couldn't change anything there. My thoughts and prayers were with those families. But I needed to make a difference!

I felt that I needed to resolve to help insure that such an incident would not happen in my community – Greenwood, South Carolina. I obviously couldn't do it alone, but I needed to work with my fellow citizens toward positive change. We needed to be moving away from hatred and intolerance. Every community wrestles with teen pregnancy, drugs, violence, and poverty. But what have I done to help?

Only now do I realize that the stage was set for this personal "inquisition" about five years prior. I was at a hospital fundraiser listening to a health care futurist, Leland Kaiser. Leland Kaiser is no ordinary futurist. He demanded that hospitals take a much more active role in their communities outside of traditional healthcare. While some of the audience rolled their eyes over his somewhat evangelical approach to his message, I found myself in rapt attention. He had a message for me though I have to admit that it took me several months to really hear it and understand it.

"For anything that happens in our community," Leland Kaiser said, "each of us as individuals and your hospital as an entity need to say, 'I am the problem, I am the solution, I am the resource.'" Those were pretty simple words but the message was powerful for me. I have to take personal ownership in the issues in my community (I am the problem), I have to work with my fellow citizens (I am the solution), and I need to be willing to devote my continuing energies to the community (I am the resource). Those 12 words have become my mantra and catapulted me headfirst into community activities since 1994.

As a geneticist and pediatrician, I've always felt that I was making substantial contributions to the community. But was I really contributing as an individual or was I contributing as a physician keeping my "proper professional distance?" When I answered the question honestly, I knew it was time to roll up my sleeves and really get involved. Numerous projects subsequently occupied my community activities, and I was active and involved. Then Columbine happened in April 1999.

So what else could I do? I was active, but was I making a difference? I typically have not been the kind of individual that writes articles for the newspaper, but I felt inclined to do so after Columbine. In the process of writing the article, I found myself trying to come up with specific action items for myself and for my fellow citizens. In that initial article, I considered five action steps to make a positive difference in our community.

1) Learn to be the best parent you can be

Parenting is the toughest job in our lives and is always an on-going process. We can always improve our parenting and consequently our children. Parenting is the key to having good citizens.

2) Get involved

Remember the words of Leland Kaiser ("I am the problem, I am the solution, I am the resource") for what is happening in our community.

3) Stay involved

Sometimes it's easy to get involved but true commitment means staying involved. Be willing to adapt to change and be part of the process.

4) Love for others

Intolerance, hatred, and poor conflict resolution will not exist if we exhibit love for others.

5) Forgiveness

We need to be able to forgive others for their mistakes and forgive ourselves for our mistakes as we move forward. Without forgiveness, we are stuck in a cycle of inadequate conflict resolution never moving forward.

In the five years after the Five Steps were initially laid out, I have discussed specific action items under each of these steps. Many of these articles have been archived on the Five Steps website, **www. fivesteps.org,** for the interested reader.

If you use a pentagon to symbolize the Five Steps and then connect all the steps (because they are all interrelated), we see a star. I'd like to see this star as illuminating the steps and the path to follow for positive community improvement.

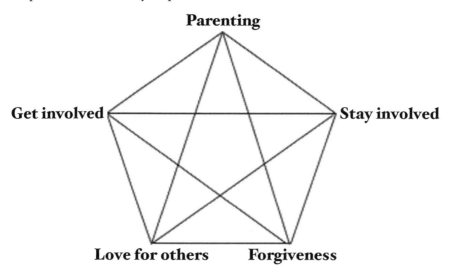

In retrospect now, I can see that I have been on a journey that I had not anticipated when I started my career as a geneticist/pediatrician. This journey is important, and I also know that I am not in charge. I willingly accept the role that seems to be evolving.

As I do that, I continually look for inspiration from various sources (church, friends, and family). One of those most significant sources of inspiration in my life has been the wisdom of my mother. It is unfortunate that you often don't really understand the wisdom of our parents until they are gone. Such is the case with my mother.

At the memorial service for my mother in December 2002, my brother read the following words, penned by my mother in 1968, that are still true today:

Dear Father in Heaven, every night as I strive for sleep, my mind accelerates to a fast pace, and then I feel I must write what I feel.

Today, as I read about the Vietnam War, and all the brave men fighting to make the world a better place to live in, the civil rights stress, and the death of the great Martin Luther King, and the tremendous rebellion's of today's youth, and drugs becoming an everyday nightmare – all these distressing things, plus the mad scramble for just survival and trying to conquer adversities which are with us daily – I wonder what we can do as individuals to try and make the world a much better place to live in?

This can be achieved, (and it will be a slow process), I pray, with the bettering of our own individual lives. For when one person betters himself morally, and spiritually, and emotionally, he, in turn, can influence the power of good over evil, kindness over cruelty, and love, the most important of all, over hate, bigotry, and just a general not caring at all attitude. Each kind word and act will help. The more we think of others, and how we can help them, the less selfish we become, and the more we try each day, we can't help but bring the power of the love of God to others.

Let us work as though we were one cog in a machine that works exceptionally well, and soon we have more parts that are operating better, and eventually the entire machine is perfect. I realize that this sounds too idealistic, but the thought could be put into operation, and even though evil still exists, it would lose quite a lot of its potency, and eventually maybe even die out completely, at least brought down to a minimum.

Help me as a person, who is constantly searching for betterment in myself, to give and try daily, to do my part, at least as well as I'm able. Believing in the strength of God's love, I feel will bring me closer to being stronger myself, and thereby maybe influencing another to do the same.

I see that the Five Steps I have proposed are based on the wisdom and guidance of my mother. An admittedly imperfect woman, she surmounted significant obstacles in her life, to provide the sound basis for my nurturing and my parenting.

We are now many years post Columbine. My journey continues. I realize that I can make a difference. I hope we can all make a difference. If you substitute "we" for "I" in the words of Leland Kaiser, the twelve words now read – We are the problem, we are the solution, we are the resource. We can change our communities, one neighbor and one neighborhood at a time. It is not our traditional role as physicians – or is it? The more I think about it, it is. It is absolutely our job! We have the opportunity to help heal the mind and body of our community in addition to our patients. I look forward to this on-going journey and encourage your participation.

Five Steps, 2013

These first two chapters have now set the stage for the discussion of specific issues under each of the Five Steps. It is my fervent hope that the discussions can stir some interest and action in the readers, especially the parents, to work on specific items that can make a difference.

It brought the nation to its knees, but now that we've gotten back up how have things changed; what have we learned?

(inscription from the wall of the Columbine Memorial)

Section 2

LEARN TO BE THE BEST PARENT YOU CAN BE

Chapter 3

Breastfeeding

Breastfeeding is one of the most important steps we can take for our children, but as a country we do a dismal job of promoting it. And, frankly, I've been no exception. As a general pediatrician for more than twenty-five years, I was an advocate for breastfeeding, but I admit I didn't give it the energetic support it deserves.

Our children have paid the price for the lack of emphatic support. Too few babies in South Carolina and Greenwood County are exclusively breastfed for six months, and few continue to receive breast milk exclusively until twelve months of age. That's a real shame, and I wish I could have pushed for it more.

Well, here's my second chance.

Readers in different states can check the "Kids Count" (KidsCount.org) report to see unique data for their area. They will find that, while some states do better than others, too many of our children are getting a poor start in life. We can't start too early to support our children, and no option comes earlier than the decision about the way they are fed.

Breastfeeding is one of the most significant nurturing acts that a mother can do with and for her children. Other support providers (father, grandparents, other family members, and friends) can further assure that mothers are given the necessary daily support (such as housework, meal preparation, and required rest) that they need. The physical and emotional act of breastfeeding—cuddling an infant while supplying the nutrients of life—has to be one of the most heartwarming scenes we can visualize. A baby who receives the optimal nutrition and the physical and emotional nurturing of being breastfed by his or her mother starts life the right way, and is provided the right example of nurturing for the years to follow. There is good evidence to suggest that enhanced early brain and child development supports healthy brain-wiring (see Chapter 19).

Breastfeeding: A Decision Before birth

Because breastfeeding is as important a decision as the manner of birth, the commitment to breastfeeding should start prenatally. Breastfeeding represents the optimal nutrition for babies, and breastfed babies are less likely to have severe gastrointestinal problems and respiratory problems, such as ear infections. Breastfeeding does not require refrigeration, and it is the most economical way to feed a baby. Additionally, breastfeeding:

- provides better nurturing for infants,
- decreases the risk of allergic disorders for children,
- decreases the risk of obesity in childhood,
- might enhance the neurodevelopment of our children (better IQs), and
- could change blood cholesterol in adolescents, leading to a decreased risk of heart attacks in adults.

Mothers who breastfeed decrease their own risks for breast cancer, diabetes, and obesity. Plus, it has been estimated that if 90% of US infants breastfed for at least six months, the cost savings to society would be $13 billion per year.

What are the long-term benefits to children who are breastfed? I think there is a greater likelihood that the child will be read to, a greater likelihood that the child will be first-grade ready, and a greater likelihood that the child will be nurtured throughout childhood with a decreased likelihood of abuse. I was recently intrigued to read about a study of a large group of infants from Australia. The study analyzed a group of infants and noted a statistically decreased risk of parental abuse or neglect in this group as compared to those that were not breastfed. That's right! After the investigators analyzed all of the factors, breastfeeding had a protective effect in terms of abuse or neglect.

Answering the Arguments

I should emphasize two things. First, some maternal and infant health conditions prevent breastfeeding. Second, if the best attempts at breastfeeding are unsuccessful, parents can still provide the necessary nutrition and nurturing.

The evidence is clear, however. The short term and long term benefits tell us that we should be encouraging breastfeeding 100% of the time except when medically not indicated. Yet when healthcare workers and public health workers get together to figure out how to encourage more mothers to breastfeed, many obstacles are seen and often perceived to be insurmountable. The obstacles include these arguments:

- People don't understand the importance of it;
- It's too difficult, and women want the convenience of formula;
- Women can't breastfeed and go back to work; and
- How do we get the message to everyone?

We all value our children and try to do everything possible to enhance their health. So that our children do not contract serious preventable infections, we require vaccinations. So they will get a good start on their education, we require kindergarten. If we truly valued our children, we would elevate breastfeeding to the level of importance of vaccinations or kindergarten, replacing our "can't-be-done" attitude with a "how-do-we-work-together-to-make-it-happen" attitude. We would devote the appropriate resources to make a <u>systems-wide change</u>. We would bring together government, social service, public health, healthcare, parents and hospital teams to make it happen. If we can create disaster relief plans for natural disasters such as tornadoes or hurricanes and devote resources to their implementation, we can create plans for more universal breastfeeding, to give our children the best start possible.

Why? Does it really make a difference? Aren't babies just fine with formula? Breast milk is the ideal so why not give our children the best we can? What makes breast milk so special? It was designed exclusively for babies. *Human milk is for humans.*

Are Mentors Extinct?

Parents rely heavily on their own parents (the baby's grandparents) for advice. Today, many grandmothers don't have a history of breast-feeding their own children, because breastfeeding rates fell in the baby boomer generation. We have lost a generation of potential breastfeed-ing mentors, and we need to reverse that trend. These grandmothers and other family members often want to feed the baby so they can be a part of the process. But if they want what is best for the baby, they would put 100% of their effort into supporting breastfeeding, not undermining it.

An Educational Boost

I had the opportunity to serve on the inaugural board of the South Carolina First Steps to School Readiness Initiative initiated by Governor Jim Hodges in 1999. I argued then, and I argue even more vehemently now, that the ultimate first step to school readiness should be breast-feeding. They compiled a list of risk factors that too many of our chil-dren in South Carolina experience: abuse and neglect, low birth weight, low maternal education, poverty, and teenage pregnancy. The exposure to abuse or neglect is unfortunately on the top of this list in South Carolina. Children exposed to these risk factors are far more likely to be unprepared for school.

At first the following sobering facts will seem irrelevant. But they are not:

- The "Kids Count Report" for 2012 (www.kidscount.org) estimates that 26% of South Carolina's children live in poverty.
- Forty-two percent of children in South Carolina live in single par-ent families.

- Fifty-four percent of children in South Carolina do not attend preschool.
- Seventy-two percent of children in South Carolina in fourth grade are not reading at a grade level.

These multiple factors require many approaches and significant social resolve if we are to find tangible solutions now and in the future. And let us never forget one very important thing—the one and only ticket out of poverty is education. None of the possible solutions is easy, but one is intriguingly simple. Breastfeeding should be promoted with much greater intensity.

THE TAKE-HOME MESSAGE

Any initiatives designed to help us be better parents to our children should start with the promotion of breastfeeding. It is the most natural way to improve the health of all of us. Promoting breastfeeding needs to be number one on our list of skills as parents and should be a major public health initiative!

Chapter 4

Discipline: Positive Rather than Negative

As a pediatrician, I have seen families deal with behavior problems in many ways—some good, some bad. All too often, I've seen parents "pop" their infants or toddlers with a spanking, or yell "shut up" when the child is doing what the parent doesn't want them to do. This is not effective discipline—quite the opposite. Parents need to know how to use effective discipline to encourage *positive* behavior and discourage undesired behavior, doing it in the context of a loving, nurturing relationship. Since most critical factors are learned in early childhood, these lessons need to be ingrained in the child early. Effective discipline is critical to the development of effective conflict resolution, a skill sadly lacking in our society. Unfortunately, children usually learn ineffective conflict resolution (yelling, screaming, hitting or worse) because discipline was not handled properly.

The word *discipline* comes from a root word meaning to teach or instruct. This is a very important point—discipline should be an effort to *teach* or *instruct* our children how to improve their behavior. Discipline should not be an activity to correct "bad" behavior. The American Academy of Pediatrics has published guidelines for effective discipline, noting that effective discipline contains three vital elements:

1. **A positive, supportive, loving relationship between the parent(s) and child.** For discipline to really work, this instruction must occur in an environment in which the children feel loved and secure. Disagreements and significant

emotional discord are less frequent and less disruptive in families with positive parent-child relationships.

2. **Use of positive reinforcement strategies to increase desired behavior.** If we want to reduce undesirable behavior, we must have a strategy to reward and encourage desired behaviors! Parents must be positive role models for their children in this endeavor. Children learn what they see. When they do good things, we must reward them with appropriate praise and nurturing. We must take the time to be sure we are giving them the opportunity to succeed and learn how to do things correctly.

3. **Removing reinforcement or reasonable punishment to reduce or eliminate undesired behavior.** If a child's behavior could lead to potential serious harm, swift action is needed. But the parent still must deliver this punishment in a nurturing manner that is clear to the child. Less serious behavior problems should be dealt with a calm, straightforward manner. Younger children can be placed in time-out or their temper tantrums ignored. Older children can have some of their privileges restricted (TV, time with friends or computer, driving access). Spanking or hitting a child teaches a child the wrong message (that it is ok to hit someone when you're mad) and is ineffective. Unfortunately, all too often spanking leads to child abuse.

These lessons are learned early. It is estimated that most children's consciences are formed by ages 3-5. We need to set the right example and do it the right way early.

The High Cost of Ineffective Discipline (Such as Spanking)

Ineffective discipline can be placed into one or more of the following categories:

1. **Corporal punishment**. I think it is wrong to strike a child. We strike a child when we are angry; therefore, we send

the message that is okay to hit someone when you're angry. That is not the message we want our children to learn. It is unfortunately too easy for a simple paddling to turn into something more because the parent is very upset and loses control. There is good evidence that parents guilty of child abuse were more likely to have suffered from physical punishment as children. I know some will argue that they were given "good whippings" as children, that it taught them the right lesson, and that it didn't adversely affect them. They would further point out that we need more discipline in our society. Let's use an analogy (suggested by Murray Strauss, PhD) comparing smoking and corporal punishment. Heavy smoking does not guarantee lung cancer, but it does increase the risk of death through smoking-related causes to about one in three! Similarly, most people exposed to corporal punishment do not become violent adults, but it does significantly increase their chances of using physical means to settle differences (with children, spouses, or fellow citizens) in the future. There are other ways to teach children the right message than physically striking them.

Spanking is a form of physical punishment that is misdirected in terms of its desired effect. A recent article in the medical literature (in the journal *Child Development*) provides more evidence for the negative effects of spanking. A group at Duke University studied 2,500 children (Caucasian, Hispanic, and African American) and noted that one-third of one-year olds were spanked on the average of 2.6 times per week. The unfortunate findings were that those children who were spanked had more aggressive behavior at age two and performed worse on measures of thinking abilities at age three. Other factors were analyzed and controlled for, so the spanking was the variable that made a difference—spanking of young impressionable children puts them at greater risk of aggressive behavior and diminished cognitive function.

Another recent report notes that harsh physical punishment independent of maltreatment puts children at greater risk for subsequent mental disorders. These reports do not surprise me at all. They provide more evidence against the use of corporal punishment.

2. **Verbal abuse**. I think it is wrong to yell or scream at your children. When we yell or scream when we are angry, we send the message that is okay to do that when you are angry. The other problem with verbal abuse is that it can quickly escalate to physical punishment or more serious verbal assaults (such as yelling profanities). Don't tell your children that you hate them when they are doing something wrong. Remember, you might intensely dislike what they are doing, but you do not hate them. Don't let children think that you hate them. They take that expression very literally and don't understand that you might just be blowing off steam.

3. **Inconsistency**. Parents (and grandparents) need to be consistent with their praise for desired behavior and consistent with their withdrawal of reinforcement or restriction of privileges for undesired behavior. Children will learn how to use inconsistent discipline to their perceived advantage (playing one parent against the other). We need to work hard at this and make sure they hear a consistent message.

4. **Permissiveness**. Sometimes children keep pushing and keep pushing even when they have been told that their behavior is unacceptable. We give in to their demands or fail to follow through with a reasonable punishment because we are worn out. Tough love demands that we follow through with our reasonable punishment and do what is right. But remember, you could be wrong. It is always reasonable to think again when you have reached an impasse with your child. You are the adult and expected to make a rational decision. Your child might be acting irrationally. Make sure that your assessment

of the situation is correct and your punishment is reasonable. If you're right, stick by your decision.

Greater Dangers to At-risk Children

Anger makes it difficult to control our behavior. Effective punishment can be delivered without a physical component. As I noted earlier in this chapter, some will argue that "I was spanked or paddled and I learned the right lessons when I was a child." The problem with this logic is that the majority of kids will do fine but <u>*at risk*</u> *kids will suffer possibly irreparable damage.* I don't want to take the chance because we can't tell ahead of time who is at risk and who isn't. As a child advocate, I have to assume that all children are at risk and argue against the use of spanking. If spanking damages some children in the long run, it certainly is not an effective means of discipline.

Effective Discipline Takes Effort

Discipline, as noted at the outset, should be a positive activity. Through proper instruction or coaching, our children can learn correct behaviors. Parenting is a very imperfect exercise, and we can expect multiple ups and downs along the road. Some days our instruction will be good and some days our instruction will be not so good. We need to learn how to change our own behavior if we expect to have a positive impact on our children.

Sometimes parents put their children in situations where the children will more than likely fail and then the parents get upset when they do. That is why I emphasize that parenting is a constant learning experience and it takes effort to learn how to be the best you can be.

I think many of us think that parenting comes naturally. I think many of us think that it requires no instruction. Parenting is a skill that needs constant instruction, attention, and nurturing. Today's society is complex. With all our technology and our reliance on so many factors to provide our food and shelter, it is no longer enough to think everything will just fall into place. We do not just get up in the morning, go out to the fields, raise our crops, and put food on the table. We are dependent and interdependent on almost everything that happens in the world. In addition, there are so many social factors affecting families that are beyond our control. We should not assume that everything is second nature when it comes to parenting. I argue that discipline is not an innate ability. If we take the time and expend the necessary energy to teach our children well, the need for punishment should be decreased.

Parenting is tough. Effective discipline is even tougher. Learning how to do it right is a constant struggle but one of the most worthwhile ones in our lives. Crosby, Stills, Nash, and Young in one of their songs from the 60's said to "teach your children well." Indeed, the best instruction we can give our children is effective discipline in a nurturing environment. However, there is no effective discipline out of the context of love for others and forgiveness. Always remember that mistakes will be made and together we can learn and improve our behaviors. We're never too old to learn and improve.

THE TAKE-HOME MESSAGE

We need to optimize the environment that our children grow up in. It is appropriate to advocate for children by recommending against the use of physical means to discipline our children. We all pay when citizens have learned that it is okay to strike someone when they are upset and angry. These citizens have unfortunately learned to deal with emotional issues by physical violence. We have to learn to how to resolve conflict without violence. This is a lesson learned early.

Chapter 5

Bullying Should Be Tackled Head-On

"The prevalence of bullying among US youth is substantial." This quote from an article in the *Journal of the American Medical Association* reminds us of the frequency of this unacceptable behavior in our children. Physical, verbal, or psychological bullying is meant to cause physical or mental harm, and it occurs over a prolonged period of time. The authors sampled more than 15,000 students in grades six to ten during 1998. Close to 30% of the students reported moderate to frequent involvement in bullying: thirteen percent as a bully, ten percent as one who was bullied, and six percent as students who both bullied and were bullied. Not surprisingly, those children who bullied others or experienced bully behavior tended to have greater difficulties with psychosocial adjustment than their fellow students.

The journal *Pediatrics* previously published an article on a study of bully victimization during the first years of school in a group of more than 2,200 children born from 1994 to 1995 in the United Kingdom. The children were assessed at five years of age and at seven years of age for behavior and school adjustment problems. The authors analyzed the differences between these age groups in two sets of victims: one group of children who were victims of bullies and one group of children who were victimized by bullies, but who also bullied other children. The first group (pure victims) comprised 14% of all children and the second group 6%. More than 20% of all five-year-olds were victims of bullying.

Name calling, physical harm, or exclusion from games for a variety of reasons (such as having only one parent) were some of the forms of bullying, and immediate psychological consequences such as bad dreams, abdominal pain, or school avoidance were noted. The disturbing results of this study show that both groups of victims demonstrated more behavior and school problems at age seven, even when allowances were made for underlying problems the children had at five years of age. The authors conclude that early-school-year victims of bullies are more likely to have maladjustments. They rightfully note that the mental health of children might be significantly affected by this problem. Subsequent studies have shown that victimization can lead to mental health problems in adulthood. Adults with mental health problems are more likely to have personal or social interaction issues that can affect their ability to lead a fulfilling life. Personal or social problems affect our interactions with others, since it's tough to get involved with positive community change when you're busy dealing with your own problems. And unfortunately, some victims of early childhood bullying might contribute to antisocial behavior that is destructive to the community and counter to the ideal of exhibiting love for others.

Victims of bullying have perpetrated some of our most infamous school violence episodes, so action is definitely indicated. Schools are thrust to the forefront of dealing with bullying. Out of necessity, they must adopt a strict code of no-tolerance, but often that policy does not address the serious mental health issues that are present. Society must accept some responsibility for attitudes (such as media images and value system) and circumstances (such as poverty or inadequate parenting) that lead to this behavior. Society must take a holistic approach, dealing with all the related aspects of this problem. We cannot just take a no-tolerance approach without acknowledging and attempting to correct associated issues.

What are the solutions? I suggest ways to get involved in the process:

- Don't accept bullying as a normal adolescent behavior. Recognize it as abnormal behavior that needs to be dealt with. Let's change the mindset that accepts too much of this behavior. Bullying is never innocent and can lead to significant problems;

- Know your child's mental health. If your child is a bully, a victim or a bully-victim, she needs your help because she is at significant risk. Intervene!;
- Push the education system in your area to adopt school-wide anti-bullying policies;
- Study effective programs that have been used to combat bullying; and
- Recognize that we need to work together: public health, health care, mental health, education, parents, and faith organizations.

The above studies should tell us something. Close to one-third of our children are harmed by bullying, whether they are the bully or the one who is bullied. Both groups of children need help learning to deal with effective social behavior. Most of that help should start at home.

I think a significant percentage of children affected by bullying learned the behavior at home—that is unacceptable! As parents, we must demonstrate effective social behavior. We should not use physical, verbal, or psychological threats toward our children that are out of proportion to the lesson to be learned. We need to remind ourselves how impressionable our children are, at every age. Bullying, by anybody, is unacceptable.

THE TAKE-HOME MESSAGE

We cannot bully our children if we expect them to avoid similar behavior. Bullying in the schools is a real problem. Know your child's behavior. If they are experiencing bullying (as bullies or being bullied), take appropriate steps to help them. They need your attention. Bullying doesn't just affect a few of us. It affects all of us. We need to take positive steps to deal with this complex problem. We can make a difference when we recognize that it is our collective problem.

Chapter 6

Know the State of Your Child's Mental Health

One of the most difficult aspects of parenting is understanding the mental health of our children. Parents tend to concentrate on their child's physical health—growth, colds, fevers, and gastrointestinal problems, to name a few. But learning how to interpret a child's mental health (moods, reaction to good things, reaction to bad things, ability to adapt to change, ability to deal with progressive changes in school, and ability to react to environmental and family crises) is critical to being the best parent you can be. As parents, if we don't know our children's mental health, we are leaving them vulnerable to outside influences that more often than not aim them in the wrong direction or leave a lasting scar on their psychological development.

Some estimates state that as many as one in thirty-three children experience depression, and possibly as high as one in eight adolescents. These kids do not live in a void. They often experience depression in a context of a depressed parent or depressed close family member. Adults who are depressed are less likely to provide the nurturing environment that children so desperately need. Parents and children function as a team. If children are depressed, the team does not function well. If parents are depressed, the team does not function well.

Additionally, a recent study documented that adults who are depressed are less likely to break a cycle of alcohol abuse or drug abuse. If you don't think that depression touches your life, think again. Even if you or an immediate family member have never had signs or symptoms of depression, think about the major events in our society that have occurred when individuals with depression have used firearms to express their rage.

Critical Warning Signs

The warning signs that parents should be alert to include sadness, withdrawal, hopelessness, having trouble in school, or significant changes in sleep or eating habits. If parents have concerns, they should seek appropriate assistance in a loving, caring way. If someone breaks an arm, they get appropriate care. If somebody has depression, they should get appropriate care without feeling ashamed or being snubbed by their friends, neighbors, and loved ones.

Equally important is for parents to recognize the signs of depression for themselves and seek appropriate care. Parents who are depressed cannot nurture their children in the best way possible. Because so much of children's significant development occurs before the age of three, if a parent is depressed and is unable to interact and care for children in a loving way, it will have serious consequences. Families should recognize the early signs and symptoms of depression and seek help as needed.

Avoiding Other Forms of Abusive Behavior

The abuse of children by a football coach at Penn State (and other events in the past, such as the Catholic church scandals, the judge who was recorded whipping his daughter with a belt during a profanity-laced tirade, and horrific bullying stories) should remind us that children need our constant attention. Their mental health, as manifest in many ways, can give us vital clues as to how we should interpret their behavior and respond in a loving, caring manner.

We place trust in many people in our society, as well we should. It frightens us, disappoints us, and ultimately can repulse us when people we have revered act in a less-than-honorable way toward our children. The morning of this writing I read an op-ed piece by Ross Douthat in the *New York Times* that struck a chord. He notes that good people can do wrong by not intervening when they should, even though they did not do anything legally wrong. He wrote that "good people, heroic people, are led into temptation by their very goodness—by the illusion, common to those who have done important deeds, that they have higher responsibilities than the ordinary run of humankind. It's in the service to these 'higher responsibilities' that they often let more basic ones slip away...[Some convince] themselves their institution's good works mattered more than justice for the children they were supposed to shepherd and protect."

Douthat concludes, "Not even a lifetime of heroism can make up for leaving a single child alone, abandoned to evil, weeping in the dark."

What's my point? Just as parents need to know their child's mental health, our "communal parents" also need to know the mental health of the children around them (See Chapter 9). Communal parents are one's extended family, teachers, doctors, close friends, neighbors, and folks with significant contact with the life of our children. If these adults have concerns or see things that adversely affect the lives and behavior of our children, they have a moral obligation to seek the advice of the appropriate people, and those contacts may not stop with the parents.

THE TAKE-HOME MESSAGE

When children are adversely affected by words, deeds, or events in their lives, they often manifest those hurts by exhibiting significant changes in their behavior or mood as a result of alterations in their mental health. Parents and their other social protectors need to respond, listening to them in an effective, loving, and caring way. Addressing the issues at the root of the problems is also important. These steps are crucial to improving the lives of our citizens and our community.

Chapter 7

Reading as an Early Necessity and a Public Health Issue

Early stimulation for infants and toddlers is critical for their development! "What else is new?" you might ask. We all know that, but I don't think we really have addressed early stimulation programs as well as we need to. I think we assume that if children haven't received the optimal stimulation and parenting, we can correct problems when they enter the school system. We couldn't be further from the truth.

Scientific evidence clearly shows that learning ability and personality traits are developed before the age of three years. This is long before children enter school. We cannot wait until they enter the school system to address these issues. Whether someone drops out of high school or not depends very heavily on their early development. Parenting in today's society does not come naturally. Whether we earn $2,000 per year or $200,000 per year, we all need assistance.

Reading is probably the most important skill of childhood (and children do grow into adults). In addition to breastfeeding, reading is an important and vital component of the child's development process. We need to place our emphasis on reading as a significant early childhood development issue.

Read Stories—Even in Utero

Start reading to your child while they are still in the womb. "Is he crazy?" you might ask. You bet I am. I am crazy about reading. Parents who read to their children prenatally will continue to read to their children after the baby is born. Children are born to read, but will only read if the parents work with them.

What else can a parent do after birth? Read every night to your children. Quiet time around bedtime can be one of the most positive parenting experiences, providing for a quality interaction between child and parent. Besides, the right books can help instill the right values in children. You can also use the daily newspaper, going over letters and words from the headlines to encourage children to read. Go to the library for the adventure of getting a child a library card, and make a trip to the library part of your weekly routine. Children and parents reading together are learning together. Do it today and everyday.

When addressing a Senate committee on January 24, 2002, First Lady Laura Bush noted that "Reading is the keystone for academic and life success" and a vital component of successful early cognitive development. "A failure to learn to read not only leads to failure in school, but portends failure throughout life...Reading failure does not just constitute an educational issue—it reflects a significant public health problem. And, with great anguish we note that parents who cannot read cannot engage their own children in reading activities."

THE TAKE-HOME MESSAGE

Instilling in our children the habit of reading is a vital part of parenting. Reading is also a public health issue and should be promoted as such. Reading should get emphasis from parents, health care providers, educators, and our public health officials. Reading is the ticket to the future for every child and the key to an educated community.

Chapter 8

Never Too Old to Be a Positive Role Model

We should always strive to be the best parents we can be. We're never too old to learn how to improve this skill—and it is a skill that deserves practice! The dictionary defines parenting as "the raising of a child by its parents." While none of us will dispute that technical definition, I think all of us know that parenting means so much more than raising a child in today's volatile, challenging, often threatening society. Many, many books have been written about parenting. Everyone has their own ideas. As a pediatrician since 1979, I have seen parents who are doing an excellent job, and I've seen parents who need quite a bit of help. Sometimes it's very easy to give advice, but very difficult for families to follow that advice, given their set of circumstances.

The demands of making a living and raising a family in such a mobile and increasingly technology-dependent society can create multiple problems for any parent. And some parents start the process with added problems – teenaged parents or single parents, for example. Their stresses can compound the challenges in trying to be a parents and taking care of themselves. We should never assume that parents don't need help navigating the maze that we call parenthood. Over a quarter of a century of pediatric practice and being a parent myself have emphasized that to me. We all need help and should never be embarrassed to ask.

The Critical Period for Parenting

As I have emphasized, the critical period when it comes to parenting is from a child's birth to three years of age. During this period, critical development occurs in a child's senses, self-image, conscience, relationships, and self-worth. You might think that some of these things occur more during the school years, but there is overwhelming evidence to show that the early years are essential ones for the development of children, their future educational success, and their well-being. Our ability to properly nurture and parent our children in these early years is the primary determinant of our children's futures. Some folks, unfortunately, don't understand this.

I recently read an article about a current popular football player. He was asked about his children, and he admitted that he was not spending much time with his children. He said that he could fix that later, and I suspect his expectation might be that he will be able to lavish them with material things as they get older. Unfortunately, he doesn't get it. Parents need to be with their children during these early years, and it is they who must provide the proper emotional support. His wealth will not buy his ability to be a good parent later. What a shame that too many people do not understand this early commitment to their children.

Many books have been written about the critical aspects of early parenting. I think one of the most important functions in parenting our children during their early years is being the correct role model. One could argue that a child younger than age three years is too young to learn from the actions of a parent, but I would argue to the contrary. How do children learn? From the actions of their parents.

Attributes of Good Parents

Three attributes that I think are critical to parenting:

- **Patience**. Parents must be patient with their children. We must recognize that childhood and adolescence are times when children learn what behaviors work and what behaviors don't work. Many mistakes will be made along the way. Patience allows us to calmly review the situation and to make decisions that make sense, not just now but in the future. Besides, patience is an excellent trait for children to emulate;

- **Persistence**. Children are constantly testing the limits of their parents' tolerance. As parents, we must persist and never give up. Persistence, when we are right, is the only option. Persistence pays off when it comes to such key activities as breastfeeding or reading to your children. Persistence pays off in monitoring what your adolescents are doing. For example, every parent should know who their children are with, what they're doing, where they are, and when they will be back. Parents can never give up, but sometimes parents need a lot of help with this persistence. Our faith, our families, our healthcare providers and our educators can assist substantially; and

- **Love**. Love is the cornerstone of parenting. Making babies is one thing, but loving and nurturing babies is something different. Our love for our children (like the love of God) should be unconditional. While we might get angry with our children and disapprove of their behavior, we never stop loving them. We might hate their behavior, but we never hate them. The compassion and understanding that are a part of love help provide the ongoing support for children and adolescents as they go through the difficult task of growing into adulthood.

I'm continually amazed at how difficult it is to be a good parent. In our free country, sometimes it seems parents are too free to be bad parents. I'm not proposing a socialized system of parenting. I am suggesting that parenting is a skill that needs constant nurturing, individually and socially. I think we should never be satisfied with the status quo with parenting, but always looking at ways to improve ourselves and get the word out in our community.

Gifts

Life is full of interesting twists and turns. Sometimes the important messages are revealed at times you least expect it. Recently, while driving, I heard Isabel Allende, noted author and daughter of a slain South American leader, discuss one of her guiding principles in life, "What you have is what you give." That is to say, the important components of your life (what you have) are determined by what you do for others (what you give). Contributing to the lives of others is the most important thing we do in our lives. This concept is a natural component of a discussion about parenting.

Learning to be the best parent possible means learning to give to your children. We give our attention and energies to our children to better their lives. But giving, in this context, does not mean the giving of material goods. Today's children receive many material things, since parents often bestow upon their children too many material things under the guise of parenting. We all want our children to lead comfortable lives, if at all possible, and we sometimes overdo our intentions to improve the lives of our children. Yet improvements in lives don't come from cell phones, Playstations, jewelry, or cars. Improvements in the lives of our children come from the *gifts of life* that we give to our children.

Here are some examples of the gifts that make a difference.

- **A good work ethic.** Whether parents work at home or away from home, they can demonstrate a sound work ethic that children can emulate now and appreciate when they grow up. Children with a sound work ethic learn to do their school work correctly. School work done correctly sets the basis for a sound education and a productive life.
- **Compassion.** Parents who exhibit compassion for neighbors and family set the right example for their children. We tend to be less compassionate toward our own families at times, but we shouldn't be. Our actions within our own family are powerful examples for our children to learn.
- **Communication.** Parenting requires significant communication. Parenting is not a dictatorship, but a process with open communication. Parents should always be the parents and make the

tough decisions and choices that need to be made, but we have to recognize that we can also make mistakes and might need to adjust our decisions. Sometimes we even have to say "I'm sorry, I was wrong." Open lines of communication allow for families to get through the tough times.

- **Living by example.** Children learn from their parents. Intolerance, hatred, and poor conflict resolution are learned behaviors. Discipline means teaching, and discipline should be always be positive. Yelling and screaming accomplishes nothing, and teaches the wrong way to deal with stressful situations. Always remember that children listen and learn from us, whether the examples they are emulating are good or bad.

Assessment and Involvement

As a childcare advocate and as a parent for the past thirty-five years, I have learned that one of the most important things we do as parents is to constantly assess what we are doing. Just because we are parents doesn't mean we know everything. Quite the contrary, we all need help and assistance in the most important job of our lives, parenting. Just because something was right one time doesn't mean it's absolutely right the next time. We have to be willing to adapt and change as circumstances change. We don't need to abandon sound parenting practices, but we should never be too inflexible. We shouldn't change just because our children want us to change. We should change because it's the right thing to do. Sometimes the tough thing to do is to change how we respond to things. And sometimes, the tough thing is *not* to change how we respond to things.

Some child-rearing experts seem to think that parents have become too involved in their children's lives. My observations over the last quarter of a century are that most of the children who get into trouble (drugs, violence, poor school performance, teenage pregnancy) don't have *enough* parental involvement. Involved parents know what their children are doing and how their education is progressing. Parents who are less involved put their children at greater risk overall.

Can parents get too involved? Sure. But I think the evidence is overwhelming that parental involvement greatly increases your chances of your children's success in education and adult life. Personally, I'd rather err on that side.

I recently read advice from one syndicated columnist who was giving one mother a hard time for helping her third grader with her spelling homework with flash cards. He said it was the student's responsibility to learn how to study. Well, maybe in high school it is, but in third grade I'd rather see a parent involved. A parent involved in third grade sets a precedent for being involved in their children's education now and in the future. Granted, our level of involvement changes as our children age, but our commitment to their success should never change. And, by the way, their education out of the classroom (what they do at night and on the weekend) demands as much attention as their education in the classroom.

Things to Learn

Parenting is definitely the toughest job we will ever have. Just as life is a continuous quest to learn how to be a better person, parenting is also such a quest. We need to prepare for parenting as early as our own adolescence and young adulthood, and then continue to improve as we progress through actual parenting of infants, children, adolescents, and young adults), and on to grand-parenting and even great-grand-parenting. You see, we never stop parenting in our lifetimes! We need to always be learning what we can do to be the best parent possible.

What are the major issues we need to learn? Well, I suggest below some of the important issues to be learned, in my opinion as a parent and a pediatrician:

- **Learn to be humble**. Humility is the perfect platform for interaction with our fellow citizens. Our children need to learn this from us;
- **Learn to be sincere**. Be honest with your children and they will learn the same;

- **Learn to breastfeed, mothers**. With rare exception, all babies should be breastfed! It's the right thing, supplying both health and nurturing to babies, mothers and society;
- **Learn the ability to change**. We must adapt to change if we expect to improve. Our needs and the needs of our children will change, and we must be ready for those changes with appropriate flexibility;
- **Learn when *not* to change**. We don't need to compromise our values just to accommodate change desired by others or society. Doing the right thing is still always the best thing;
- **Learn how to make tough decisions**. Our children need our guidance and protection. Sometimes our decisions are not popular, but hopefully they are the right decisions for their overall well-being;
- **Learn to forgive our children**. They will make some bad decisions throughout their lives, and we need to forgive them so we both can move forward;
- **Learn to forgive ourselves**. We, as parents, will also make some bad decisions. We need to forgive ourselves so we can move on and continue to learn how to be a better parent;
- **Learn to get involved in the lives of our children**. Our involvement is the key to their nurturing and future success as citizens. Reading to them, playing with them and caring for their needs are crucial early on. When they enter school, we need to know what's happening in school and out of school. When they become young adults, we can continue to provide guidance; and
- **Learn rational discourse with our children**. Do not yell at or strike your children. It sends the wrong message. Our ability to deal with conflict as adults is set in the patterns of conflict resolution we set with our children. Punishment does not have to be verbally or physically abusive to be effective. Remember, discipline means to teach, which is the most important job of parenting.

A Parental Example

When I was about ten years old, I found a ten-dollar bill on the sidewalk at a motel while our family was on vacation. That was a lot of money back then! I proudly showed my mother my new treasure, and she promptly told me that I was going to return it to the office. "Whoever lost it might be looking for it," she said. "But Mom, I found it. I should be able to keep it," I pleaded. "No son, that's not right. The right thing to do is to return it. Even if the owner doesn't claim it, you will know that you did the right thing," she explained in her proper role as my parent. She taught me to do the right thing. Even though I didn't believe her at the time, I now know that she was correct. She was indeed the proper role model for my brother and myself.

Do's and Don'ts

Parents must be proper role models for their children. Children learn by example. If parents do the right thing, children learn the right way. If children witness their parents doing the wrong thing, they learn to do the same when they grow up. Here are a few do's and don'ts for parents when they are with their children:

- Do smile and tell a stranger "hello,"
- Do treat your spouse and children with respect at all times,
- Do treat your neighbors as your family,
- Do remember that discipline means to <u>teach</u> your children, not to yell or hit them,
- Do anticipate the needs of your children,
- Do look for ways to give your children positive reinforcement, not ways to constantly badger them into submission,
- Do demonstrate good behavior for your children,
- Do the right thing even if it is unpopular,
- Do bend over backward to consider someone else's side of the story,
- Do maintain the proper perspective on events in life – God, family, and work,

- Do thank someone for an act of kindness,
- Do hold the door open for someone,
- Don't call someone an idiot,
- Don't honk at a traffic light (unless absolutely necessary),
- Don't assume someone was wrong before you know for sure,
- Don't assume you're the best just because you made a good play or won a game,
- Don't tell someone to shut up, and
- Don't yell at other people.

We could continue to expand this list of do's and don'ts. The point is that parents must always understand that their children observe their actions. Children use these observations to mold their behavior now and in the future. Parents must try to do the right things and avoid the wrong things. To be the best parents we can be, we must be the proper role models for our children!

When our own children grow up, it would be delightful to hear them say to their children (our grandchildren) "We are going to do it this way because it is the right way. That's the way my parents showed me to do things."

THE TAKE-HOME MESSAGE

The early years of childhood are critical to our future development as citizens and adults. As parents, we must be there and be cognizant that all of our actions are teaching our children. Parents are critical role models for their children. We can <u>never</u> forget that. Good parents raise good citizens and help improve our community.

Chapter 9

Communal Parenting

Isn't nurturing babies second nature to us all? Why do we need to worry about children? Surely their parents or grandparents make sure that they get what they need? Well, the answer is that a significant percentage of children aren't getting what they need! Early childhood development issues are public health issues because poor early childhood development leads to poor public health! Poor early childhood development leads to an increased risk of any of the following—drug use, poor conflict resolution or violence, teenage pregnancy, high school dropouts, and poverty as an adult. Poor development doesn't guarantee these problems, but it certainly increases the risk, while optimal early childhood development decreases the risk and enhances self-esteem.

There is an African proverb that states "it takes a village to raise a child," meaning that a local (or even broader) community of people need to work together along with a child's parents to raise children to their maximum potential. When Hillary Clinton used this proverb for the title of her book about her vision for America's children, it was dismissed in some quarters as socialist poppycock or nonsense. One retort noted that it doesn't take a village to raise a child but that it takes a family to raise a child. I feel quite strongly that it indeed does take a village (along with the family) to raise a child, and that denying this reality only prevents us even more from working together to improve our community and ourselves.

Everything that we do or hope to do is interconnected with our fellow citizens. Systems theory reminds us that we rely on each other, and depend on seemingly independent systems to function together. An example from health care is that a successful knee replacement surgery relies on multiple systems (surgeon, scientific research, medical education, operating room staff, anesthesia, nursing, pharmacy, housekeeping, physical therapy, etc) that have to function together to optimize the result. Just as a surgeon alone cannot fix a knee, a family alone cannot raise a child to his or her potential.

Let me explain the components of what I mean by a village:

- **Family**. It goes without saying that families are the primary nur-turers of children. Yet many families need assistance in so many ways, and we need to be able to provide that assistance. And—I'll say it again—we need to do a better job of promoting breastfeed-ing as the <u>best</u> way to provide primary nutrition for all children. Well-nurtured children make good citizens;

- **Medical care**. Families are not capable of independently provid-ing medical care in today's society. They rely on physicians, clinics, and healthcare systems to lead the way. Many children and their families have adequate health insurance, but far too many do not. Adequate health care for our children should not be an issue in our society, and I am embarrassed as a health care provider that so many children and families cannot access proper care. To be raised properly, children need optimal health care. The return on invest-ment for providing this care is far greater than allowing health care costs to escalate and the health of all children overall to decline. Healthy children make good citizens;

- **Education**. Children absolutely require the best education pos-sible. For the less fortunate in our society, the only true way out of poverty is through education. Education opens new avenues for advancement for all of our children, whether they are heading to the military, to the job market, or to an advanced degree. Education is also an obligatory tool to enhance parenting. Education should teach us tolerance for others and acceptance of the many ways in which we are different, yet really alike. Educated children make good citizens

- **Recreation**. Children need more exercise and our community needs to ensure that we have the proper vehicles for that—community centers, school programs, after-school programs, sport and non-sport recreational programs. Active children make good citizens;

- **Law enforcement**. Our law enforcement system needs our full support. They need to able to adapt in a proactive (rather than a reactive) manner to seek ways to improve our community. At the same time, we need to recognize that supplying the opportunities for improvement in our community are not somebody else's responsibility. We have to take responsibility for tangibly improving our community. Law-abiding children make good citizens; and

- **Church support**. Folks who are active in their religious organizations know that they have a responsibility to nurture all of the children of the church. As a Presbyterian, I have accepted the responsibility to provide Christian nurture to the children in my church. In the family of God, we all work together. Spiritually-led children make good citizens.

I'm sure that we could expand on the list above when it comes to naming ways that we are all interconnected and need each other. This interconnectedness is what makes us so successful when everyone and everything works together. This inter-connectedness also has the capability to tear us apart as a community, for when one system fails, the whole system is likely to fail.

Note the common thread above—children who are helped by different segments (or systems) of our community can grow up to be good citizens. Without these inter-connected systems working together, we cannot make the progress that we need to make in order to improve the lives of our children, our lives, and the life of our community.

Well, I have to admit that I am frightened at how the current political climate is affecting our children. Programs that affect the well-being of children and their families (health services, mental health services, and education are at the top of this list) are being cut back at a time when families with few means are struggling. The cutbacks will have the unwanted effect of making things worse. I quite frankly see a two-tiered system becoming more prominent than ever before. The folks with less means will become the folks with lesser means and poorer health going forward. For such a great country, it is hard for me to accept the current trends in fiscal "responsibility" that are put in place to the detriment of our citizens. To deny the fact that the most vulnerable in our society continue to suffer the most is to deny the plight of poverty affecting so many people!

One more thing worries me about our children. At a national pediatric meeting in 2011, I heard evidence stating that 60% percent of children in the USA are exposed to violence. I'm not talking about the type of violence shown on video games. I'm talking about real violence such as assault, robbery, maltreatment, sexual abuse, or witness to significant violence. It is well known that exposure to violence in the early years puts children at risk for adverse behaviors and poor coping skills later in life. When children are exposed to violence (and its concomitant hatred), they learn adverse ways to deal with the inevitable conflicts in life. If we can handle conflict resolution well, society benefits. If we cannot handle conflict resolution well, we all suffer the consequences. We need better systems in place to protect and nurture our vulnerable children.

When we fail our children, we fail our communities and ourselves. We have a communal responsibility to all of the children in our communities. Stated another way, we are communal parents for all children. I have previously quoted the words of Leland Kaiser in Chapter 2 who emphasized that any problem in our community is a problem for all of us. He states, "I am the problem, I am the solution, I am the resource" to remind us that everything and everyone is connected. All of us have a communal responsibility to work together to improve our lives. Without that, we cannot improve as a community. And as a life-long pediatric advocate, I argue that such a burden is even greater for our children, because they represent the next generation.

THE TAKE-HOME MESSAGE

"It takes a village" is not just a nice saying. When times get tough, our responsibilities to our children are even greater. Cutting back on services and resources and just hoping that children can pull themselves up by their bootstraps is wrong and denies our role as a communal parent for all of our children. We cannot improve our lives and the life of our community if we don't take personal responsibility for everything that happens in our community related to our children.

Chapter 10

Gun Control

Gun control is always a controversial topic. Opponents to gun control argue about our constitutional right to bear arms. Proponents argue about the risk of guns in the hands of people who are not mentally stable and who might use them for the wrong purposes, such as in the Columbine High School and other tragic shootings. Opponents often site a bumper sticker that states "Guns don't kill people. People kill people." It is not my intent to resolve the gun control controversy, but to address the issue of sound gun management for parents.

A recent article on firearm injuries and deaths noted the following statistics for children and adolescents younger than the age of fifteen. These statistics are compared to other industrialized countries. The United States has a:

- firearm homicide rate sixteen times higher,
- firearm suicide rate eleven times higher, and
- accidental firearm injury rate (serious injury or death) nine times higher

These statistics tell me that our most fragile citizens (our children) do not have enough protection from these potentially life-ending instruments. Parents must instruct their children about the dangers of firearms and protect them from the inappropriate handling of firearms. Children also need to know that firearms are not used to resolve conflicts in society. This point cannot be over emphasized enough. Firearms are only to be used for self-defense, hunting, or law enforcement. They are not to be used when you are angry or depressed. If they are used when somebody is angry or depressed, all the wrong things can and will happen. Firearms have no place in conflict resolution!

Any firearms that are in the house must be locked up and the ammunition placed separately. Children must be protected from them. We do not leave poisons out for children to drink, so we shouldn't leave firearms out that can have equally devastating consequences. Proper education about firearms should be included in our public education system in addition to our home instruction.

THE TAKE-HOME MESSAGE

Parents must instruct their children about proper use and the danger of firearms and protect their children from firearms. While gun control in our society is being debated, there should be no debate about gun control in the home. It is an absolute must!

Chapter 11

Fatherhood and Self-Discipline

Multiple articles in the lay press discuss the problems that often arise within single-parent families (and absentee fathers) in low-income and minority households. This problem is substantial. Kids Count data in 2008 documented single-parent families in my home region, Greenwood County, South Carolina. The percentage of children between the ages of one and seventeen in single parent families in Greenwood County was 34%! That's an astounding statistic. It demonstrates a significant problem, in that at least one-third of the children do not have the guidance of two parents, and I would submit that two parents are critical to the nurturing of our children.

Divorce also contributes to single parent families. In families affected by divorce, often times the father's role is decreased and limited to certain time periods. I know this from personal experience. My parents divorced when I was nine, and my father was in and out of my life. His interactions were limited. He tried to play a role, but certainly wasn't there at critical times when I needed direction that my mother could not solely supply.

Yet it is naïve to think that just because a parent is around, he or she will necessarily be an excellent parent or role model. Parenting requires work. It requires training, it requires patience, and it requires constant reassessment. Remember that one of the most critical parts of parenting is discipline, and as we should continually remind ourselves, discipline means to teach. The discipline of our children should always be a learning experience and always in an environment of love. We may hate certain behaviors of our children, but we should always love them unconditionally.

On Father's Day, 2008, I clipped a *USA Today* article by Oliver "Buzz" Thomas, a minister, lawyer and author. He has some great advice for all of us fathers:

- Fathers do not have to suspend good judgment to have a close relationship with their children;
- Fathers should not try to win affection. They should earn it;
- Be the father for your children first. Being a pal is not enough;
- "The best dads discipline themselves first, their children second." I love this sentiment. Fathers should analyze their behavior, which manifests in their words and actions. These behaviors should be steady and consistent, providing instruction in a loving, caring environment. Only when fathers discipline themselves first can they learn how to teach their children the right way to move forward. Only then can they really be the proper examples for their children. As we have previously stated, when fathers are right they should continue along that path. But fathers can be wrong. When we are wrong we should acknowledge that, and alter our course accordingly; and
- Buzz Thomas ends his article with a poignant bit of wisdom. He states, "I've yet to meet a dad in his 70s who said, 'I wish I'd spent more time at the office,' or a child who said, 'I wish my dad hadn't spent so much time with me.'" You can't get time back. Savor the time with your children. Teach (discipline) yourself first, then teach (discipline) your children.

THE TAKE-HOME MESSAGE

Healthy communities need caring citizens. Caring citizens were nurtured appropriately by their parents. Caring citizens will grow up to try and improve the lives of their fellow citizens and their community. Parenting is a crucial step to improving our community, and fathers are an integral part!

Chapter 12

Resilience

One day as I was driving, I heard an interview with T. Berry Brazelton, MD. Dr. Brazelton is a well-known pediatrician whose career has spanned six decades, and dozens of books about child development and behavior. During his interview, he highlighted something that resonated with me. He noted, "I think the biggest thing a parent can give a child today is resilience—helping them see they have the inner resources to overcome whatever they have to."

Wow! Isn't that interesting! A leading expert in childhood development after six decades of service states that resilience is the biggest thing that parents can give to their children. Since we know that life has its ups and its downs, parents need to learn how to help their children deal with the downs. There is an old adage that states a person is defined not by their handling of good times but by their ability to handle life's difficulties. The ability to overcome adversities is the resilience that Dr. Brazelton was talking about. Failure in childhood is not only inevitable, but also part of the growing process that leads to enough resilience to deal with the downs of life. Without resilience, we lack a basic skill to lead a productive life and to contribute positively in our communities.

But how do we give our children the resilience that they need? Let me make some suggestions:

- Remember that the critical time for childhood development is before three years of age. Our attention to the love and nurturing of our children during this period sets the stage for their emotional, social, and personal development. I cannot overemphasize the importance of this time and the need for constant attention to the needs of our children;

- The quality of the education we offer our children defines their ability to lead productive lives. Education is crucial for our children, but let's not forget that academic education is just one component of the overall education of our children. Parents and other adults provide the bulk of the education of our children at non-school times. We need to be ever mindful of that;
- Parents serve as constant role models for their children. How parents handle adversity defines the way children handle adversity when they grow up. We need to have the same resilience that we're trying to teach our children;
- Children need to learn how to resolve conflict peacefully when they are young. The hallmark of conflict resolution is forgiveness. A great deal of resilience has to do with appropriate conflict resolution and learning how to forgive; and
- We need to provide our children with the inner resources that Dr. Brazelton referred to. These inner resources come from our early parenting and then from the consistent support during childhood that also provides appropriate limits. Providing our children with the appropriate inner resources is not pampering. It's doing what parents should be doing.

THE TAKE-HOME MESSAGE

Resilience is a crucial trait to be nurtured in all children by their parents. It allows us to be able to handle adversity in a positive way. Citizens in a community also need resilience to be able to improve our community when things are not always going well. That's what defines our ability to make a difference!

Chapter 13

Lessons from "Annie"

I absolutely love musical theater. Indoctrinated at a young age by my mother, I love to feel the stories, hear the music, and let the spirit of the entire production take over.

The musical *Annie* particularly inspires me. The story of Annie revolves around an orphan and her search for her parents. As I watch, listen, and feel the entire production, I realize that each of the musical numbers in this heart-warming tale offers valuable lessons about the different virtues present in parenting. Let me review the parenting lessons contained in the musical numbers in *Annie*. Below, there is a brief description and then the lesson for each of the musical numbers.

- **"Maybe"** (Annie wonders what her parents are doing and when they will pick her up.) Children need to know that their parents will always be available to help them and comfort them, from birth to and through adulthood. If natural parents cannot fill the role, other folks need to.
- **"It's the Hard Knock Life"** (Annie and her orphan companions lament the horrible conditions in the orphanage.) Tough conditions and stress in life have a unique impact on children, far greater than we often realize. We need to anticipate the special needs of children, instead of just assuming that they will be fine.
- **"Tomorrow"** (Annie's view of the positive things to be found in each new day in spite of adversity.) Optimism is one of the finest

traits that parents can exhibit. Even in tough times, the grace of God provides eternal hope.

- **"I Think I'm Gonna Like It Here"** and **"Something Was Missing"** (Annie has just been introduced to all the luxuries in her new home, and Daddy Warbucks has learned that something was missing in his life in spite of all his wealth.) Children (and adults!) are easily influenced by material goods. We need to remind them about the really important things in life—the ability to love, to nurture, and be nurtured.

- **"You're Never Fully Dressed Without a Smile"** (A radio commercial for toothpaste.) A smile for your children and a smile for others sends a powerful message about your caring for other people. Smile and mean it!

- **"NYC"** (A show-stopping number about New York City, its apparent harsh reality and its vulnerable caring side.) Parents often have to do tough things on behalf of their children or make difficult decisions for their children. Yet they need to handle these issues in a loving, caring manner, not in a dogmatic, "because I said so" way. When parents deal with these tough issues, they can appear to be stern or uncaring, much like the way many people perceive New York City. The events of September 11 and Hurricane Sandy have shown us that apparently cold or stern environments such as New York City are capable of responding to catastrophic events in the most heart-warming manner. Similarly, parents are capable of doing the same, and maybe we should drop our often-present "tough" facades as we deal with each other and certainly our children.

THE TAKE-HOME MESSAGE

Life "sings" in music and song! Powerful lessons await us, even in our entertainment, if we listen and learn from the events around us. Parenting is the toughest job in our lifetimes. Let's remember to comfort our children, help our children adapt to stress, be optimistic, keep our proper perspective, smile, and remember we are here for our children and each other. My thanks to "Annie!"

Chapter 14

Happiness for Our Children

Parents always have dreams for their children. "Will she become President? Will he become a sports superstar? Will she be healthy? Will he marry and have healthy children? Will she be happy?" This latter question, about happiness, is probably the most frequently asked question and is the predominant dream of all parents. We want our children to be happy.

I remember when I was growing up, my mother frequently told me that I should do whatever I wanted as long as I was happy. "As long as I was happy" seemed to be the key phrase. Her dream for me was to be happy. I think part of this instruction to me was based on parental guilt, that as a single mother she felt that her best attempts at parenting were still short of the ideal. Nothing could be further from the truth.

Well, I adopted the same goal as I entered parenthood. I wanted my children to be happy, not necessarily successful, adults. I now realize that I was very short-sighted and the isolated, abstract goal of happiness is not what parents should aspire to for their children.

What is the right goal? I think the right goal for parents to seek for their children is for them to be nice people. *What did he say?* Yes, I think that if our children grow up to be nice people, we will have been truly successful parents. No matter what walk of life, no matter what economic status, no matter what job status they reach, people need to learn how to be nice to each other in all their interactions. I used the word nice in the

sense of caring, loving, sharing, and helping. People who have these attributes will be happy! There is no doubt about it!

People might think that they might be happy just by achieving their
financial goals or by their professional success. These people are not necessarily nice people. If they have achieved their goals or successes without
caring, loving, sharing, and helping along the way, they are not nice people.
Nice people can be paupers or millionaires. Nice people are made happy
with the fulfillment of helping others, not as a result of their wealth or
success. One of the dictionary definitions for happiness is "the feeling of
pleasure or contentment." It's nice people, indeed, who have that feeling.

THE TAKE-HOME MESSAGE

I think parents should aspire for their children to be nice people.
Parents, therefore, need to do everything in their power to achieve this
goal, constantly teaching our children the importance of helping others.
By helping others, we are improving their lives, our lives, and the life of
our community. Our children should be nice people, and then they will
be happy.

Chapter 15

Childhood Obesity

Childhood obesity has become a national adult health problem. The problems of adult obesity (cholesterol problems, hypertension, heart disease, diabetes, depression, sleep apnea, orthopedic problems, and gastrointestinal problems) are now occurring more frequently because of the rising rate of both childhood and adult obesity. These health issues consume the bulk of our health dollars, yet we are not adequately addressing these issues at the most important time of prevention—childhood! If we are serious about dealing with health problems in our society, we have to tackle them in children with the help of parents and schools.

What is the scope of the problem? The ratio of weight to height (body mass index [BMI]) serves as a measure of obesity and takes into account size. A BMI of greater than the 95th percentile for age is considered overweight or obese. A 2003 policy statement from the American Academy of Pediatrics on childhood obesity notes that about 15% of children between six and nineteen years are overweight or obese. The prevalence of overweight and obesity is also on the rise for children younger than five years. Children and adolescents today are less active than in previous generations, and less active children are more likely to have problems with weight, high blood pressure, and diabetes. It is estimated that childhood obesity will persist into adulthood for 20% of overweight 4-year-olds and 80% of overweight adolescents.

The critical periods of development for excessive weight gain are infancy and adolescence. In infancy, breastfeeding is known to be a protective factor (that is, the longer the duration of breastfeeding, the less the risk of obesity). Therefore, bottle fed babies have an increased risk of obesity in the years ahead. In adolescence, less physical activity and worsening nutrition (more soft drinks, more fried food, fewer fruits, and vegetables) have contributed substantially to problems of weight control and are a signal of problems that can carry into adulthood.

The crucial first step to controlling our nation's weight problem is parenting. Parents need to recognize the problem in society and take steps to avoid it in their children. Parents need to serve as positive examples for their children and address their own weight problems. Further, parents need to avoid labeling their children. Information and guidance regarding weight issues need to be nonjudgmental and blame free. Significant emotional problems can be associated with being overweight (or even underweight). Dietary moderation and increased physical activity are the key tools that parents need to use for their children.

What other things can we do?

- More children should be breastfed! As a matter of fact, <u>all</u> children should be breastfed when possible. This should be the primary prevention tool for obesity in our society.
- Recognize weight problems so that they can be handled sensitively in order to encourage children and their families to deal effectively with them.
- We need to encourage healthier diets, especially in schools. For example, soft drinks should be eliminated from schools and school-sponsored activities. Only then can we send the right message and show that we mean it.
- Physical activity should be a greater part of our life style. Physical education has a significant place in the education of our children. Active people are healthier people.

THE TAKE-HOME MESSAGE

Learning to be the best parent you can be means teaching your children healthy ways of living. By effectively dealing with overweight and obesity problems, we can help shift valuable resources away from expensive health care related to obesity problems to needed community projects. Healthier citizens are more productive and involved citizens!

Chapter 16

"S" Words that I Hate and Love

One of our goals as parents is to teach our children to be courteous and respectful of others. Courtesy and respect are reflected in words and deeds. I want to concentrate on some words to avoid and some words to embrace.

There are certain words in our society that are appropriately considered distasteful and should be avoided (though we have all slipped at one time or another). I'm sure we can all come up with a list of such words to be avoided. When we hear these words uttered by our children, we take a variety of steps to prevent such a recurrence in the future. I'm also sure that one of those words we do not want our children to say is the "s" word. I think you know which word I mean. But let me tell you a story that I heard recently.

A five-year-old boy came running to his parents after being with a group of older boys. He exclaims, "Mommy, Daddy, those boys used the "s" word!" His parents are glad that he recognizes that the "s" word should not be used and reinforce that to him. He then replies, "I know they should not have called the other boy stupid!"

The "s" word that this young child recognized was not the one his parents had anticipated. Instead of the classic "s" word, he felt that stupid was a word that should not be used to describe other people.

My Short List of "S" Words to Avoid

- **Stupid**. Whenever we call someone stupid, we demean others and place ourselves above them. There is no place in rational discourse for words that belittle people. To say "You're stupid" to another certainly doesn't help as we try to work together for the common goal of community improvement. There are other more diplomatic ways to express one's displeasure for an apparent lack of understanding.
- **Shut Up**. I think that this expression is one of the rudest expressions in our society. It's never used in a positive manner and only serves to raise negative emotions or feelings. Parents should never tell their children to "shut up." There are other ways to ask people to be quiet without being mean.

My Short List of "S" Words to Embrace

- **Sorry**. Seeking forgiveness for misdeeds in our daily lives should be a frequent occurrence. We need to be able to ask forgiveness and extend forgiveness. Saying "I'm sorry" with honesty is one of the most humbling things that we do, yet, at the same time, is one of the most loving things that we do.
- **Sincerity**. Sincerity is not a word that we necessarily use in conversation, but one that should be the backbone of all of our interactions with others. We should always be sincere (honest, truthful, without pretense) as we deal with each other. It's often hard to do, but worthy of our continued effort.

THE TAKE-HOME MESSAGE

Our words and deeds define our ability to work together for the common good. Let's be mindful of our choice of words and our actions so that we can move forward, not backward. Demeaning or belittling remarks have no place in our interactions with our families and friends. Let's only use good "s" words!

Chapter 17

Limiting Screen Time

Yes, too much television and computer can be detrimental to your child's health! There is good evidence to suggest that too much TV in infancy and early childhood and too much computer and video game time later on can negatively affect the fragile early nervous system development of children. Two recent articles in the journal *Pediatrics* address these issues.

One study looked at more than 1,000 children at 1 year of age and again at 3 years. Their time spend watching television averaged from 2.2 hours per day at 1 year of age to 3.6 hours per day at 3 years of age. Some children had considerably more TV time (four hours or more). The researchers then looked at the same children at 7 years of age and noted the children with more TV time were more likely to have attention problems. The attention problems included such things as difficult concentration, easy confusion, impulsivity, obsessions, and restlessness. These problems are suggestive of the same problems seen in attention deficit/hyperactivity disorder (ADHD). Ten percent of children with early TV viewing had attention problems, the same percentage for ADHD in our school-age children.

An accompanying article emphasizes the influence of environmental exposures (such as television) on the developing brain. These influences can alter the eventual maturation of the "wiring" in the nervous system. While the study mentioned in the paragraph above has not proved that early TV viewing causes attention deficit/hyperactivity disorder, there is good reason to limit TV and other viewing, given the current evidence.

The American Academy of Pediatrics recommends no screen time for children younger than two years and no more than one to two hours of quality television per day for older children. Some studies have shown that over two thirds of children younger than two years watch TV for more than two hours a day, and some more than four hours a day!

With the possible association of television and attention problems later in childhood, we should limit TV in our younger children. We should take a proactive stance to protect our children and enhance their learning abilities. We can spend more time reading with our children or other direct activities instead of letting them sit in front of the TV or computer. We might be able to stem the rising tide of attention deficit problems requiring special behavior control and often medication in our children. Healthy children who are ready to learn, are less likely to have significant school problems when they grow up.

THE TAKE-HOME MESSAGE

Because parenting is the toughest job we'll ever have in our lifetime, we often have to make difficult and often unpopular decisions for our children. Let's reverse the trend of too much TV, computer, and video game time in early childhood, and replace it with more parent time. More involved parents and their children help build a better community.

Chapter 18

Listen to and Learn from Your Children

Learning to be the best parent possible is a never-ending task. One of the most significant parts of good parenting is listening to your children. When I say listen, I mean use information from our children to learn how to improve our parenting. Children can teach us valuable lessons if we listen to their messages. These messages can be humbling as we realize our own mistakes and our need to improve.

Let me share with you some things my children have taught me about myself. Corrective actions are suggested in the parentheses.

- Sometimes I am wrong. (I need to be willing to acknowledge this.);
- Sometimes I have to make tough decisions that are not popular. (That's ok. That's my job.);
- Sometimes I am too inflexible. (I need to be willing to adapt or change.);
- Sometimes I don't live up to my promises. (I need to be careful about what I promise. If I don't fulfill a promise, I need to have an alternate plan.);
- It's the little things that matter. (Play with your children, read together, go to their activities. Spend time with your children!);
- A parent's job is unconditional. We should always love our children. We don't have to love their behavior. (We do not have to tolerate unacceptable behavior. As a matter of fact, it is our job to

change it, <u>at the same time</u>, reminding our children of our love for them.);

- Sometimes when I am very mad, I feel like hitting someone. (While this is a natural reaction, I need to refrain from hitting my children. Hitting children when you are angry sends the message that it is ok to hit someone when you are angry. That is the wrong message for our children.); and
- I can't just say "Because I said so!" (I need to know why I am saying something and be able to explain it.)

THE TAKE-HOME MESSAGE

Parenting is the toughest job in our lifetime, but also the most rewarding. We have a tremendous responsibility to our children to do the right thing. In the process of parenting, we must listen to the messages from our children and improve ourselves accordingly.

Chapter 19

Toxic Stress in Children—It's Real and It Hurts

Our society has a communal responsibility for our children, so parenting is a social responsibility. It is imperative that we have systems in place to assure maximum development for all children and especially those at high risk. Children raised in poverty, in single parent families, or with few educational opportunities do not need handouts, but they need policies in place that allow them to grow into health during their early childhood. Such policies eventually allow for systems to be put into place that can make a lasting difference. Never underestimate the power of policy makers to set the right processes in motion!

We know that the most important developmental period in the lives of our children is before the age of 3 years—before they enter the public education system. As a child advocate for many years, I am saddened to see disparities between children in families that are at increased risk and children in families that are at less risk. In my estimation, we can do much better, but I don't see the resolve in our society to really improve the situation, given our current political climate and financial difficulties. Yet I see no greater need than our aggressive support of young children in their early years!

To explain what I'm talking about, we need some background. The American Academy of Pediatrics, the professional organization of pediatricians dedicated to the health of all children, recently initiated a massive effort to understand how early brain and child development affects the lives and well being of all children. Their exhaustive effort in conjunction with known science and researchers has resulted in many findings:

- Brains are built over time, prenatally to young adulthood;
- Brain architecture is built in a cumulative, bottom-up manner;
- A dynamic interaction between genes and experience shapes the architecture of the developing brain;
- A solid foundation in brain development is required to support future skills;
- Brain development requires the integration of social, emotional, and learning skills;
- Creating the right conditions in early childhood is more effective and less costly than addressing problems later in life; and
- Child development is the foundation for community and economic development.

Given these findings as background, it has been noted that less than ideal circumstances in early childhood can lead to toxic stress in all children, but particularly high-risk children. The presence of some stress may be a normal part of life, but it is crucial to have support systems in place that give children the ability to handle stress.

Three types of stress have been identified: positive, tolerable, and toxic.

Positive stress is a normal response to a situation that is brief and relatively mild. Examples include frustration in young children, receiving immunizations, or starting at a child care center. With supportive relationships, positive stress is a part of normal development.

Tolerable stress is associated with a greater degree of magnitude such as the death of a family member, a divorce, or a natural disaster. These circumstances can be quite disruptive and can cause excessive reaction in children. However, these reactions are less likely to have long term consequences if proper protective adult relationships are in place.

Toxic stress occurs when strong stressors (child abuse or neglect, parental substance abuse, and maternal depression) are not well buffered by a positive adult relationship. It has been shown that toxic stress can affect brain development in an adverse way. Abnormal brain development has long term effects, some of which are not readily reversible.

The reason toxic stress gets its name is because it is truly damaging to the developing child. There is significant evidence to support this. Toxic stress can:

- Affect the levels of stress hormones in the body that disrupt the developing brain architecture;
- Affect one's responses to life's events, such as having increased fear or anxiety;
- Change brain development in a way that will cause some children to respond to events in an exaggerated and often inappropriate manner;
- Increase the lifelong risk for developing a variety of adult-onset diseases, such as cardiovascular disease; and
- Set in motion the process of passing some of these effects to subsequent generations by altering the DNA and the triggers that turn genes on and off.

The above points highlight two critical issues—toxic stress plays an important role in the trans-generational passage of health and educational disparities and the origin of many adult health outcomes originate in early childhood.

Because we know that toxic stress can disrupt brain architecture that will alter the foundational basis for learning, behavior, and health, it's time to figure out a way to tackle these issues head on! Toxic stress occurs primarily when there is a lack of social-emotional buffering. Therefore our efforts should involve helping the children, their families, and our society. We have a communal responsibility (each and every one of us) to understand this problem and to be a part of the solution. It requires a combination of personal involvement, community will, and social policy, as well as an understanding and acceptance of our common humanity.

The American Academy of Pediatrics has outlined a public health approach to toxic stress. First, universal primary preventions (such as anticipatory guidance, high quality early childhood care, and consistent messaging) can be significant factors as we recognize the potential effect of toxic stress for all children, not just those who are at risk. Second, for those at risk, screening and targeted interventions (such as home visitations, Head Start, and early intervention programs) can begin to provide more directed assistance. Finally, for the symptomatic children affected by toxic stress, evidence-based treatments are necessary. But key to these processes is the recognition that toxic stress is real and deserves the attention of all of us.

THE TAKE-HOME MESSAGE

Toxic stress is real. Toxic stress hurts our children. Toxic stress hurts adults. Serious problems can be averted if we have the resolve to acknowledge the problem and deal with it in a communal way to improve the lives of our citizens and the life of our community.

Rather than a loss of innocence, I've got to hope that something like this encourages us to be better people.

(inscription from the wall of the Columbine Memorial)

Section 3
GET INVOLVED

Chapter 20

Participating in Community Organizations

We lead such busy lives that it's difficult to imagine what we are able to do individually to make a real change in our communities. Our tendency is to hope that community leaders such as elected officials will pass laws and set up programs that lead to positive change. We often say, "I sure hope they can fix that problem," when we hear about troubling situations in our community and society. However, the only way change can occur is for *us* to become personally involved. We have to accept individual responsibility for problems. We can do this by participating in organizations that can make a difference.

Effective Change is Grassroots Change

Effective change occurs one block at a time. Groups of residents can meet their neighbors, exchange ideas, prioritize projects, propose solutions, and implement plans for the neighborhood. These activities empower neighborhood leaders to build on local assets, accepting responsibility for encouraging and enabling the rest of the neighbors to reach their full potential, melding neighborhoods into a thriving community. Truly effective change in our society only occurs at the grass roots level. It cannot be mandated from governmental agencies.

Schools as Neighborhood Associations

Are schools a type of community or neighborhood association? Absolutely! As a matter of fact, they represent an association in its best form—a group of individuals gathered to promote the best interest of the overall group. The proper education of our children is vital to the survival of our society. We entrust our children to an outstanding group of professionals (teachers, principals, therapists, counselors, and other educators). But guess what? They cannot do their best job unless we are involved with the education process—involved as parents, involved as citizens, involved as mentors, and involved as voters. Here's how to become involved in schools:

1. Take an active part in your child's education, working with your child daily;
2. Take an active part in your child's education, working with the teacher in the schools;
3. Volunteer to be a mentor. Mentoring is a prime example of individual commitment to help another person and therefore society as a whole; and
4. Support innovative thinking. Consider using schools as neighborhood resource centers, where formal education is only one component of the range of services available.

Public education is successful when there is a true collaboration between parents, schools, and other members of society. All of us have a vested interest in public education, not just those of us with children in schools. The neighborhood associations that convene in our schoolhouses everyday represent the ultimate grass roots effort for community change and the improvement of the quality of life. Get involved—one student at a time and one school at a time. It will make a difference.

Poverty, the Environmental Toxin

Why is educational involvement so important? I had the opportunity to attend a workshop that highlighted the work of T. Berry Brazelton, MD (see Chapter 12) who is considered one of the foremost developmental pediatricians in America. One of his associates, Dr. Steven Parker, presented a talk entitled *Double Jeopardy: The Impact of Poverty on Early Childhood Development.* "The developmental costs of poverty for children are excessively high," he said. "Approximately two-thirds of children who tested mildly retarded have grown up in poverty. The cost to society can be measured in terms of school drop out, unemployment, delinquency, unwanted pregnancies, and inter-generational perpetuation of failure." Dr. Parker went on to discuss poverty as an "environmental toxin," noting that if poverty were an infectious disease, it would be considered one of the worst epidemics known to mankind.

The age-old question, then, is what do we do about poverty? We have been tackling the issue for decades, without significant success. In my lifetime alone, there have been many unsuccessful wars on poverty. Dr. Parker feels that the only real ticket out of poverty is through education. Approximately 40% of those without a high school education live in poverty, in contrast to the 9% of those with a high school education who live in poverty. The education of our children starts at birth and does not finish even in adulthood. We need to emphasize, at every age, the importance of education and become involved in the education of our children, whether we have children in the school system or not.

Faith-based Organizations

Involvement in faith-based organizations is one way to become involved. In Chapter 4, I discuss discipline, which stems from the root word meaning *to teach or instruct.* Disciples (pupils or followers) of their religion should be willing to spread the good news of love and forgiveness in the context of proper respect for all religions in our community. We are these disciples! We should not be afraid to practice what we learn in church, temple, mosque, or other religious settings.

What do I mean by becoming active in faith-based organizations? I'm talking about embracing the teachings and practicing the message by becoming committed to the activities of one's place of worship. Many parishioners are silent participants in their church activities. That might be suitable for some activities, but most of them require some degree of physical and emotional involvement for these activities to really make a difference for the faith-based organization and its parishioners. Be willing to be humbled. There is no better way to understand the message of our religions.

Involvement also calls for a willingness to take the messages of our place of worship into the community, translating it into tangible work. We can and should perform loving acts of kindness for the less fortunate. These are the humanitarian acts that define our loving nature. All denominations also have the opportunity to band together to weaken the root causes of misfortune—poverty, illiteracy, intolerance, violence, and drugs, to name a few. We should not wait for government agencies or schools to correct these problems. They cannot. We can, but only if we work together, as people of faith. With all the faith-based organizations in our community, we should be able to make incredible strides toward community improvements that make a difference.

A Whimsical Definition of Involvement

Involvement means many things to many people, and each individual contributes in his or her own meaningful way. I highlight some of the important aspects of involvement using each letter from the word.

I   It has to be a "first person" activity. **I** (not they) will get involved. Remember "I am the problem, I am the solution, and I am the resource."

N   We cannot take "**No**" for an answer. Tangible change is always possible.

V   **V**olunteer. Part of our duty as citizens is to volunteer and to help each other.

O   **O**ut-of-the-box thinking. How often do we hear that certain things can't be done? New and innovative solutions to problems always exist if we really put our minds to it. There's a wise quote from the ancient East: "He who thinks it can't be done should get out of the way of those who are doing it."

L   We have to **L**earn how to get involved. I don't think it comes naturally. The skill has to be developed.

V   Always remember that the work of community improvement is extremely **V**aluable. Community improvement helps all citizens and generations to come.

E   It takes personal **E**nergy to get involved. We must be ready to sustain the effort.

M   We need to be **M**entors, **M**obilizers, **M**otivators, **M**onitors, and **M**ediators in our community. All of those **M**s serve us well as we do our best to make a difference.

E   **E**xcellence. We should always pursue excellence as we target the goal of community improvement.

N   **N**urture your relationships within the community. The only way we can make a positive difference is to work with our fellow citizens.

T   Remember, **T**eamwork is the key. While one individual can spark an idea or lead a group of people, the work cannot get done without the team.

THE TAKE-HOME MESSAGE

We must get involved in the neighborhood, educational, and faith-based activities in our communities. They are vital to our self-interests and the interests of our community. Learn about what is happening in each of these organizations and how to get engaged. The work of citizens cannot and often will not be done by other people. Only you and I can do it by being part of the solution and investing our resources, beginning with our time and commitment.

Chapter 21

Heroes Get Involved in Their Communities

Our society has a tendency to apply the term hero to folks it considers perhaps worthy of praise. Sports stars and their physical accomplishments are examples of those who don't often fit the dictionary definition of hero: a "man admired for achievements and noble qualities." My own personal definition of hero describes an individual who selflessly devotes his or her time and talents to the betterment of others, without fanfare, i.e. someone who is always there to help.

One such hero was my dear friend, Dr. George Brumley, a pediatrician from Atlanta, Georgia, who died, along with his wife and three of their five children and spouses and many of their grandchildren in a tragic plane accident in Africa. As I look back and reflect on the impact Dr. Brumley had on my life, I note the many roles George played as he was continuously helping the rest of us.

Researcher. Dr. Brumley's work was at the forefront of research into the lung disease that affects premature infants. When I was a pediatric resident in the 1970s, many premature infants died of this lung disease. We now take for granted the chemical (surfactant) that is used to prevent the life-threatening lung disease. Because of the work of Dr. Brumley and of many others, this chemical is now readily available and saves many lives.

Teacher. Dr. Brumley was an excellent role model as a teacher. He was always available to instruct young doctors-in-training like me, praising our strengths and gently pointing out mistakes so that we could continually improve our skills to help others.

Friend. Even though he was my professor, Dr. Brumley agreed to attend the delivery of my eldest son as a favor to me. He continued to be my friend in the many years that followed.

Administrator. Dr. Brumley was the chair of Pediatrics at Emory in Atlanta after he left Duke in the early 1980s, and used his administrative skills to guide this prestigious program until 1995. During that time, he also served as interim dean of the medical school.

Mentor. Dr. Brumley was always available to provide sage advice to me throughout my career.

Philanthropist. Dr. Brumley paid back to the community, through church, the arts, education and community projects.

Innovator. He was instrumental in developing several key programs in Atlanta (after his "retirement"!). These inner city health and education initiatives serve as testimonials to his vision and his determination.

Disciple of God. Dr. Brumley was devoted to the Word of God and the work of church, never losing sight of the most important thing in life.

Dr. Brumley was <u>involved</u> in significant projects in every phase of his life. He was a true sage to his fellow man—a motivator, a mobilizer, a mediator, a monitor, and a mentor. Yet Dr. Brumley never sought personal credit for his accomplishments. He insisted that the credit go to the team around him—his family, his colleagues, and his fellow citizens. He was, and is, a hero.

THE TAKE-HOME MESSAGE

To make a difference in improving our community we must get involved. With a real hero, Dr. George Brumley, as an example, we must *continue* to get involved in different projects, at every stage in our lives.

Chapter 22

Graduation, Social Capital, and Involvement

Every year, in the spring, young men and women graduate from high school. From there, they pursue further studies in college or technical schools, careers in the military, or employment in the community. Some also start their families at this time (the most important job of their lives!). These pursuits are vital to our communities, our state, and our country. Every year at graduation ceremonies, the young adults are told about their responsibilities, that their freedom in this country to pursue their field of choice is a privilege, not a right. They are told that they are no longer passive participants in our society. They are now citizens. And the main responsibility of citizens is to get involved.

Graduation implies the completion of a certain process or stage. More importantly, graduation signals the start of the next process or stage in life. The adjective "gradual" means advancing by incremental steps. This definition embodies what I consider graduation—the completion of a certain stage (such as high school), assisting us as we advance in life by incremental steps. The logical extension of this line of reasoning is that we never really graduate! We are continually (gradually) advancing in life. And the important lessons along the way are to learn how to improve our lives and the lives of others. Whether we are students, parents, or grandparents, we are always progressing and learning, and we never really graduate. There are always lessons to learn, and there is always more progress to be made. We are just commencing the next stage of our lives, hence the alternate term for graduation, "commencement."

Too often we think that our elected officials will make a difference. We elect representatives to establish policy. Yet policies only matter if the citizens are actively involved, working to improve their community, putting those policies into effect or working to modify them as appropriate. Our elected officials don't do the work of improving our community. We do. They are important as policy makers, but citizens make the difference. We are our own social capital in that we exhibit the good will, friendship, sympathy, and social interactions to move things forward.

Social Capital

Robert Putnam's book, *Bowling Alone: The Collapse and Revival of American Community,* emphasizes the term social capital to refer to involvement in our community. Initially described by a school supervisor (L.J. Hanifan) in 1916, social capital refers to "those tangible substances [that] count for most in the daily lives of people: namely good will, fellowship, sympathy, and social intercourse among individuals and families." Communities with social capital "may bear a social potentiality sufficient to the substantial improvement of living conditions in the whole community. The community as a whole will benefit by the cooperation of all its parts, while the individual will find in his association the advantages of the help, the sympathy, and the fellowship of his neighbors."

A careful reading of the above quote notes the following:

- It is not sufficient to do things in a void. We must get involved with and for our fellow citizens.
- Involvement in our community helps the community as well as the individuals. This is a classic win-win situation.
- Good citizens are active participants in the community.
- The benefits to the community from individual actions are often greater than the individual actions themselves.

- Involvement leads to interaction and to a subsequent understanding of the issues affecting the lives of our fellow citizens. Our individual actions (whether positive or negative) affect others in our community. With involvement, we learn to appreciate the reactions to our actions, which leads to cooperation.

Robert Putnam further notes that social capital:

- allows citizens to resolve collective problems more easily
- greases the wheels that allow communities to advance smoothly
- widens our awareness of the many ways in which our fates are linked
- improves individuals' lives through psychological and biological processes

Wow! If social capital is so good and can help our community, why can't we just work together and make it happen? Because it requires involvement, *sustained involvement. We must get involved and stay involved in many ways.* Our involvement will help our community, our fellow citizens and ourselves. Perhaps it is too idealistic to think that we can all make a difference, but it makes perfect sense. We are the only ones who can make a difference.

Dr. Putnam points to a significant decrease in social capital in American society since the mid-1970s. He provides substantial evidence that we have decreased our collective participation in the following areas:

- Political. By service or by voting, we are less actively involved. "We [are] reasonably well-informed spectators of public affairs, but many fewer of us actually partake in the game."
- Civic. "Americans have been dropping out in droves...from organized community life."
- Religious. "Americans are going to church less often than we did for three or four decades ago, and the churches we go to are less engaged with the wide community."

- Workplace. "Americans are demonstrably less likely than our parents were to join with our co-workers in formal associations." He emphasized that the workplace does not appear to be "the salvation for our fraying civil society."
- Informal social connections. "A very wide range of activities [over] the last several decades have witnessed a striking diminution of regular contacts with our friends and neighbors."

Many of us have suspected a nationwide drop in community involvement. What do we do about it? We can be cynics and just complain *or* we can try to reverse the diminishing social capital. Dr. Putnam notes that Americans went through a similar cycle before and made positive changes. He also reminds us that social capital "allows citizens to resolve collective problems more easily...[social capital] greases the wheels that allow communities to advance smoothly...[social capital] improves our lot by widening our awareness of the many ways in which our fates are linked... [and social capital] operates through psychological and biological processes to improves individual's lives."

In other words, without social capital, we do not have a chance to really improve our lives and the life of our community. One example is that Dr Putnam's work has shown that community and parental involvement in education can improve the educational performance of children more effectively than higher teacher salaries or smaller classes. Active participation makes the difference.

How can we get involved so that we can make a difference? The following is just a partial list of suggestions:

- Vote. Study the issues, learn about the candidates, and vote;
- Join a civic organization and participate;
- Participate in the activities at your child's school;
- Get involved in your church and its activities;
- Connect with your co-workers;
- Join or start a neighborhood association; and
- Watch less TV and read more.

As we discuss our responsibility to others, getting involved and social capital, I'm reminded of a famous song from the disco era, "Stayin' Alive." I have to admit that I don't know the lyrics to this dynamic song by the Bee Gees and immortalized in dance by John Travolta in the movie *Saturday Night Fever.* All I know is the beat and the title. The lively beat of the song and the title remind me that at every stage of life, we need to "stay alive" by getting involved in improving our community.

Let me close this chapter with a poignant example of the advantage of social capital from Dr. Putnam's book. He describes two men that are members of a bowling league. A 33-year-old white member agreed to be a kidney transplant donor for a 64-year-old African-American member. That arrangement would likely not have occurred had they not been members of the bowling league, connected in a social organization that broke down barriers and encouraged interaction.

THE TAKE-HOME MESSAGE

Involvement is the key to positive change in our community. We must get involved and stay involved in social activities and community affairs to make a real change. Let's get reconnected and stay connected.

Chapter 23

Elders as Sages

Bill Cosby, the famous comedian, makes some very pertinent observations and delivers them with an enjoyable wry sense of humor. When addressing the graduates at Ohio State University, he told them—"I want you to listen to [the] elders in your family. Listen to them. They love you. Don't listen to your friends. They only know what you know. When they [the elders] decide to tell you about life, it's an act of love toward you."

Young adults are sometimes cocky enough to think that they (and their friends) know all that they need to know about life. Cosby reminds us that young adults, as they enter the world of involvement (employment and parenthood), need to listen to the advice of their elders. And the elders need to get involved as their sages. Sages are elders who choose to use their life experiences for others' benefit.

In 1900, 2.4 million Americans, or 2.4% of the population, were older than 65 years. In 2011, approximately 14% of the population was older than 65 years. This aging population represents a wealth of resources that we need to use effectively in the decades ahead. Our aging citizens might be losing some of their physical capabilities, but they still can be vital contributors to society.

A recent book entitled "From Age-ing to Sage-ing: A Profound New Vision of Growing Older" by Zalman Schachter-Shalomi makes a dramatic case for the need of elders in our society. He notes that in past generations, elders were considered to be tribal leaders or wise individuals who lent significant advice to the younger generations. With the advent of the industrial and computer revolutions, we seem less likely to listen to the advice of our elders, assuming that they don't know anything, because they might not be familiar with some of the latest technology. The author, however, emphasizes that elders are:

- sages who offer experience, balanced judgment and wisdom for the welfare of society;
- wisdom-keepers who have the ongoing responsibility for maintaining society's well-being and safeguarding the health of the planet;
- people who are still growing, still learning, and synthesizing wisdom from life-long experiences, formulating this into a legacy for future generations; and
- going through a process of conscious and deliberate growth, becoming sages who are capable of guiding their families and communities with hard-earned wisdom.

Often we treat our senior citizens as our elderly not our elders. Despite the loss of some physical and mental capabilities, our elders should come to terms with their declining physical capabilities and accept expanded mental potential, spiritual renewal, and greater social usefulness. Effective sage-ing is a process that enables older people to become spiritually radiant, physically vital, and socially responsible elders of the tribe.

Our elders (sages) are, most of all as also discussed in the book, capable of being:

- **Mentors.** Mentoring is perhaps one of the most important roles of elders—that of actively supporting and nurturing the educational process. Hands-on mentoring can make a difference when it comes to issues such as literacy, teenage pregnancy and parenting just to name a few examples.
- **Mediators.** Elders help to resolve conflict, both civil and intergenerational. Our elders have a world of experience to help with issues that cannot seem to be resolved.

- **Monitors.** Elders serve as watchdogs of public bodies. Their world of experience can help recognize problems in their early stages and advocate for change before significant harm is done.
- **Mobilizers.** Our sages can use their experience and influence to spearheading social change, leading the fight for positive change. In Greenwood, John Drummond and Marion Carnell are prime examples of local leaders who are sages and mobilizers.
- **Motivators.** Elders urge people toward the public good and away from special interests. It is too easy to get caught up in our narrowly focused agenda, losing sight of the common good. Elders can help keep us on track.

Two mentors during my medical training, Dr. Sam Katz (former Chair of Pediatrics, Duke University Medical Center) and Dr. George Brumley (see Chapter 22) are constant reminders to me of the example I need to live up to as I age.

The actor Kirk Douglas wrote an article in *Newsweek* titled "What Old Age Taught Me." In his nineties, he and his wife have used their acquired wealth to build 400 safe playgrounds in Los Angeles, establish a home for homeless women suffering from addiction, support his namesake high school with a financial incentive for all the graduates, and establish a theatre for young artists. His actions are a testimonial to his ongoing involvement as a sage in his community. He has mentored, mediated, monitored, mobilized, and motivated many folks with these projects. He also rightfully acknowledges that there is something greater than these actions. "The greatest dividend to old age is the discovery of the true meaning of love," he proudly states. He has listened well to the lessons of life and advanced his knowledge (his sage-ing) into actions that can make a difference. The subtitle for the article is "Now in my golden years, I've learned that you can't learn how to live until you know how to give." I couldn't agree more. I just wish we all, including myself, learned it sooner.

THE TAKE-HOME MESSAGE

It is never too late to get actively involved in our community, promoting projects that will improve the lives of its citizens. We cannot accomplish positive change without a willingness to listen and learn together. Our elders have a responsibility to get involved in the events of today. They cannot sit back, saying it is no longer their responsibility. It's their responsibility because so many of their generation sacrificed their lives for their opportunities, which are now our opportunities. I'm looking forward to the challenge in the years ahead.

Chapter 24

Teachers Affect Eternity

Henry James, one of the most important American authors writing in the late 1800s and early 1900s, said, "A teacher affects eternity: he can never tell where his influence stops." Truer words have never been spoken. We can all reflect on our lives and see the influence of teachers in our lives—in our ability to learn, our social skills, our community activities, and in our assurance of their love for us.

Perhaps in my emphasis on the importance of senior citizens (or sages) contributing to our society, I have underemphasized the importance of teachers and the five Ms of teaching (Chapter 23). Let me correct that by highlighting teachers and the five Ms of teaching:

- Teachers are our motivators. They understand the need to push us to learn, to encourage us to be eager about learning. Learning is not just something that is accomplished in grades 1 through 12. Learning is a lifelong activity, and the impetus for that learning has to occur in our early years of instruction;
- Teachers are our mobilizers, directing our energies in a positive way, equipping us to get engaged in society. Teachers can truly "light that fire," can get us going in so many different directions, so that we are positive contributors to society when we are adult citizens;
- Teachers are our monitors. We will not always do the right thing. Teachers can be there to help correct our actions and guide us

through the complex maze that is the process of learning right from wrong. None of us is perfect; that's why we need instruction;

- Teachers are our mediators. Oftentimes we find ourselves engaged in some type of conflict, minor or major, that needs resolution. Teachers can help us see these conflicts clearly and work through these issues. Conflict resolution is one of the most difficult issues in our society and needs constant attention and further bolstering. Teachers can indeed be the mediators of this process; and
- Teachers are our mentors, there to help guide and lend a steady hand to our development. Whether one enters the work force or pursues higher education after high school does not matter. The important thing is that we proceed down those paths in a positive way. Teachers can be role models and sources of guidance as they direct students.

Teachers play an important role in our society. Parents are, of course, the primary teachers. Yet I think public school teachers are sorely under-appreciated. The ultimate teacher whom many of us look up to is Jesus Christ. Those who follow the Christian faith are students of His instruction and responsible for spreading His Good News. His instruction has truly affected eternity.

THE TAKE-HOME MESSAGE

As we work together to improve our lives and our community, let us cherish the contributions of our teachers. Let us remember that teachers affect eternity. Their involvement in our lives and their influence never stop. Look at the teachers around you and say thank you. If you are a student, accept their instruction and be a better person from it.

Chapter 25

Get Involved for Children—They Can't Vote

Children cannot vote. They should not be allowed to vote, for obvious reasons. Yet more often than should happen, we are caught up in partisan battles, and children's interests are rarely well served. Every four years, when the race for president dominates the headlines, we hear lots of promises from incumbents and candidates about how to correct the problems of neglected, impoverished and abused children in our society. As a pediatrician, I try to stay attuned to the solutions, if any, that are offered for our children. We usually hear about spending for education, healthcare, parenting and other pediatric issues. Unfortunately, when the dust settles and legislatures reconvene, it's back to business as usual with child advocates having to fight tooth-and-nail to benefit our children. Though it may sound as if I don't appreciate the efforts of these well-intentioned individuals, I do appreciate their public service, but I think that children's needs are often short-changed.

Let me give you some examples:

- We often hear that Medicare reimbursement for health services to adults is inadequate. Well, Medicaid (providing reimbursement to healthcare providers serving children and their families with significant financial needs) pays an average of 66% of Medicare rates. That means inadequate reimbursement rates (for adults) are even less adequate for children! A surgeon performing an appendectomy on a child with Medicaid insurance will receive less than a surgeon doing the same surgery on an adult with Medicare. That simply is not right. The point to this example is that inadequate reimbursement for healthcare correlates with inadequate care. Stated another way, children and families that are at highest risk for health, education and social problems are also at greatest risk of receiving fewer services, because of a reimbursement system that makes it more difficult to get quality care. Poor health outcomes unfortunately also relate to poor economic outcomes;

- The health conditions that affect adults (obesity, cancer, heart disease, diabetes, osteoporosis, stroke) *all* have their origin in childhood! What we do in childhood has an impact on our adult health. The proper care and nourishment of children's minds and bodies affects us all as adults. Let's remember this;

- If adult diseases start in childhood and reimbursement for children's services is less than satisfactory, what should we do? The answer is really quite simple; prevention is better than treatment. If we followed best practices research, we would invest more time and energy in childhood initiatives that would decrease the health burden and psychological burden of adult diseases; and

- We have to remember that, despite their promises, politicians don't do the work of improving our lives and lives of our children. We do. Granted, they set policy that can help or hinder efforts to improve the overall health of children. But the actual work to make change occurs with community-based projects, one neighborhood at a time. Improvement cannot occur without our efforts to be a part of this positive change.

THE TAKE-HOME MESSAGE

Health and social issues in childhood have a dramatic impact on adults. Since children can't vote, we need to get involved and vote for candidates who support initiatives that will have a lasting positive impact on children. But let's not fool ourselves; real change occurs because citizens in a community want to make a positive difference. We have to address important childhood initiatives in our communities because they will benefit both children and *us*!

Chapter 26

Continued Parental Involvement Is Important

The word "involve" has several definitions, but I would like to focus on two in particular: "to occupy absorbingly" (to commit emotionally) or "to have an effect on." Both definitions get to the true spirit of what it means to get involved, that is, to commit both mind and body to worthwhile endeavors. A community of caring people gets involved. They do not wait for somebody else to do the work. Oftentimes, we wait for various social or governmental agencies to mandate change and correct problems. This will not work. Real change will only occur when people get together, accept the communal responsibility for problems, and together seek viable solutions.

Parental involvement from infancy to adulthood

Parental engagement from infancy into the adult lives of children, is crucial to their children and their community.

Parents need to get involved in the lives of their children early! The first three years, as we've said, are crucial to their future development—crucial to motor development, mental development, and their future behavior, as well as crucial to the development of their consciences. Parents must make sure that their children have all their physical needs *and* their emotional needs taken care of. Physical needs (health, shelter, and nutrition) are often the easiest things to provide, yet some families struggle and need significant assistance. Emotional needs (love, nurturing, positive role models, teaching, reading) require even more work and should never be taken for granted. Children need constant attention, since these early years set the stage for later life. We need help in this process. We should never assume that it can happen automatically without assistance. Parenting means constant involvement.

Parents need to get involved in the lives of their children during the school years. Parents create a positive example for their children when they know what's happening, and are learning what they can do to make sure that their child is working as hard as possible at school. One of the advantages of getting involved in our children's school is the opportunity to relearn many things we have forgotten. Not every child can excel in every subject, but everyone can work to the best of his or her ability. Parents need to assist teachers in this endeavor. More involved parents means better students.

Parents need to get involved in the lives of their adolescents. Whenever adolescents go out, parents should know *where* they are going, *what* they will be doing, *who* they will be with and *when* they will be home. Parents need to help their adolescents make the right choices in order to avoid risky behaviors that could lead to the abuse of drugs and alcohol or teenage pregnancy and venereal diseases. These risk-taking behaviors are markedly decreased when parents are involved.

Parents need to get involved in their community. Children and adolescents need positive role models such as parents who are helping others. This is really the only way children learn how to help others.

Examples of parental involvement

Parenting is not a passive experience. Quite the contrary, it is a very active experience. Without active involvement, children don't get the nurturing and role models they need. Children learn by example and by doing. We must always be cognizant of the examples we are setting for our children.

How can parents get involved in the lives of their children? Let's review some of the ways:

- Read to your children. This is one of the most important things you can do! Learning to read is a child's gateway to the world—the neighborhood and the world far beyond;

96

- Talk to your children. Encourage them, comfort them, sing to them. Verbal interactions are crucial to developing the ability to interact with other people;
- Swap their time in front of the television and computer or video games with time with their parents. We are forgetting how to interact with each other via eye and voice contact. Texting and email are poor substitutes for direct interaction with people;
- Smile at and with your children. Children need to know that you love them. Smiles are contagious! They always send the right message;
- Play with your children. By playing with your children, you show your commitment to spending time with them, you demonstrate their importance to you, and you have the opportunity to show them how to play correctly. Children need to know how to win with humility, lose with dignity, and be courteous good sports, no matter the outcome.
- Watch your children. By watching your children, you learn about them. Watch them play as infants and toddlers to learn how to play with them;
- Go to their activities. Children are very proud when their parents come to their activities, at church or school, for example. This is the way you learn what is going on in their lives, and they see that you care. If they are performing (singing, dancing, playing sports, etc.), you can encourage them in this way. You can praise their accomplishments, you can keep them from getting discouraged, and you can correct any discourteous behavior;
- Make sure they go to bed loved. Children and parents will always have disagreements, but at the end of the day, we need to remember to hug and love our children. Don't let arguments define our interactions. Always remember to keep things in the proper perspective; and
- Be involved, even when you can't be present. We can't be with our children all the time and we can't attend all their events. But we can be involved by phone, during dinner table conversations and

bedtime chats! Find out what is happening and stay involved, even in your absence.

Involvement is the Anti-Drug

The government's National Youth Anti-Drug Campaign emphasizes parental involvement as the key to keeping our teenagers drug-free. Several key points are worth mentioning:

- Knowing what your children are doing is crucial! The National Youth Anti-Drug campaign brochure notes, "Your kids might not like your keeping tabs on where they are and what they're doing... [but] in the end, it's not pestering, it's parenting." This latter statement needs to be reiterated. You are not pestering your child if you are doing the right thing and asking the right questions. You are the parent and that is your job;
- Praise good behavior and set limits and consequences for unacceptable behavior;
- Parents need to ask a series of questions of their adolescents every time they leave the house

WHO? Who will you be with? Do you know the other children? Do I know your friends? Will there be appropriate supervision?

WHAT? What will you be doing? What will you be doing after the party or movies?

WHEN? When will your activities be over? When will you be home?

WHERE? Where is the activity taking place and where will you go from there??

It is our job to take care of our children as they make the transition to adulthood. We have to guide them through this difficult process. It's never easy, and unfortunately we will make mistakes. Often harsh words are spoken by our children and ourselves. It's our job to sort through this cloud of emotions by asking the appropriate questions and setting appropriate limits. We cannot give up. Our children will eventually understand and respect our decisions on their behalf.

THE TAKE-HOME MESSAGE

The key to healthy children and a healthy community is parental involvement, requiring time, energy, and commitment that must begin early on and continue throughout the lives of our children. Infants, children, teenagers, and adolescents all need guidance, praise, and limits.

Chapter 27

Accepting Personal Responsibility in Our Communities

We would see a major improvement in our communities if each citizen would develop a sense of responsibility for community activities. We have to remember systems thinking, which means that everything has an impact on everything and that solutions are not created in a void. Long-lasting solutions to community issues require buy-in and involvement from all segments of our community. Solutions that are not truly integrated into all segments of the community and accepted by all are not viable in the long run.

It's clear, then, that we are just fooling ourselves if we think that we can just let others or our government officials take care of the needs of the community. At best, they can assist with change, but *we need to make it happen.* The more we sit back and just let others do things, the less likely we are to effect overall positive change in our community. You'll remember that, to guide us, Dr. Robert Putnam has advanced the concept of social capital (good will, fellowship, sympathy, and social intercourse) as the glue that binds us together (Chapter 22). We need to use that glue to make things happen.

How do we make it happen? Let's look at it in a different way. In the dictionary, we can note the following attributes for the verb "involve:" *connect, affect, engage, include, and envelop.* I really like these descriptive terms! As citizens, we *connect* with each other when we get involved. We *affect* our community in a positive way with involvement. We *engage* in tangible change when we vow to get involved. Involvement is not a solo activity and when we get involved, we tend to <u>include</u> others in our efforts. We *envelop* and embrace our community when we take positive steps to improve our community.

One might argue that we cannot be responsible for everything, especially the bad things that happen. However, we do have a responsibility to help correct any problem, because this community is our community. Similarly, we cannot correct everything that goes wrong in our family, but we can commit to help with any problem that occurs. We have to—it's our family. In a similar way, this community is our family, and we need to commit to personal involvement in its affairs.

The trouble is, we tend to only get involved with issues that affect us personally. In point of fact, however, almost everything that happens in our community affects us personally and demands our attention. Even though we can't get involved with everything, we need to concentrate on areas where we can lead to the most positive change. We should not be afraid to tackle issues that are out of our comfort zone. Instead, we should broaden our comfort zone and the community's comfort zone as we try to advance positive changes.

Problems such as teenage pregnancy, drug use, intolerance, hatred, violence, insufficient first grade readiness, and poverty, to name a few, require our personal investment. In response to these problems (or opportunities for improvement), we would do well to let Leland Kaiser's words push us in the direction of *collective ownership* of the good things in our community and *collective ownership* of the things that need to be improved in our community.

Here's clarification on collective ownership:

- Collective. We must be in this together if we want to improve our community—all aspects of our community. Businesses know that they are only as good as their weakest link. Communities should operate under the same principle. We must use all of our resources to elevate all segments of the community if we are truly committed to advancing a community.

- Ownership. To own community issues means to accept them as one's personal responsibility. When we accept personal responsibility, we cannot rest until problems get resolved. Problems (or better called things that need to be improved) that are owned solely by individuals in the community and never the community itself never get resolved. They just get pushed from desk to desk.

THE TAKE-HOME MESSAGE

To improve our community, we must personally get involved by connecting with, affecting, engaging, including, and enveloping all aspects of our community. Any problems in our community are our own problems. Let's not be shy. Let's roll up our sleeves and get involved.

Chapter 28

Citizen Involvement

In the past, I have had the good fortune to hear prospective church officers describe their faith journeys, noting what they believe in and their paths to that point in time. An almost universal thread running through all of the stories is the profound impact of their parents on their lives, including the involvement of their parents in their churches and in their communities. They related childhood remembrances about going to church with their families and times when their parents got involved in various community affairs. These remembrances demonstrate first-hand the importance of leading by example and helping others.

What's my point? Getting involved is a critical part of being a good citizen and helping others. There are innumerable ways to get involved, using our unique talents to make a positive impact. In addition to helping others and improving our community, there is a significant side effect to our involvement: our children will benefit from our actions!

Parents as Citizens

The most important lessons are not what we tell our children. The most important lessons are what we show our children via our actions. Our getting involved and helping others demonstrates to our children the right way to help our community. As our children mature and progress to adulthood, they will learn from these examples, and most often they won't even consciously know it. I think that is the best kind of learning – learning by example and carrying those lessons forward in our own lives. Often it's not until we are well into adulthood that we truly realize the impact of those early lessons and role models in our lives.

As I reflect on my own mother's influence on my life, I now know that I did not consciously realize the impact of her actions until much later in my life. Her steadfast resolve to do the right thing (often against the wishes of her family such as seeking a divorce to end an abusive marriage) provided the optimal guide for my later years. I'm glad to know that I learned something from those early lessons.

Other individuals (including our fellow citizens) in the community also make a difference in our later lives. Our grade school teachers, our high school teachers, our early career mentors or our community leaders all contribute to our lives, yet the realization usually comes later—sometimes even after the exemplary individual passes away. Our ability to recognize the significant contributions of others and to acknowledge those contributions makes one realize how important social interactions and communications are to the life of our community. When we acknowledge the significant contributions of others in our own lives, we spread that word and allow for others to see such examples and learn by them.

Protecting High-risk Children

Social disparities in our country are well recognized but poorly managed. The United States recently ranked 34th in infant mortality among nations reporting to the World Health Organization. This poor rate is largely due to disparities in racial/ethnic, socioeconomic, and geographic subgroups. A recent article in the journal *Pediatrics* discusses these issues and addresses a program designed to deal with the problem.

Infants and children being raised in high-risk settings (teen-aged parents, single parents, poverty) are at risk for premature birth, decreased birth weight, child abuse, and accidental injuries. They are also at risk for health problems such as asthma and a decreased rate of school readiness. As a matter of fact, most of these issues are likely to contribute to such future problems increased drug use, increased violence, and poor high school graduation rates.

Community-based home visitation programs for first-time mothers and their children have resulted in a significant discovery; intensive home visiting reduces the risk of infant death. Home visitation programs can also decrease rates of child abuse and emergency room visits, and can lead to healthier subsequent pregnancies and the increased practice of breastfeeding. These programs now have proven results that can make a difference.

Some of you will say that this type of program seems pretty drastic and too invasive. I counter that we are currently losing the war on poverty and as a consequence are failing a substantial number of children who need our help.

I've had the opportunity to attend a pediatric CATCH meeting in Charleston, South Carolina, involving a very dedicated group of pediatricians around the state. CATCH stands for Community Access To Children's Health. There is a re-focus on children's health in society, beyond just traditional medicine. We need to make sure that we work hard to remove existing barriers to enhancing wellness—social barriers, literacy barriers, economic barriers, and educational barriers.

I was flabbergasted to hear this statistic presented at that meeting: close to 75% of children younger than 5 years are in out-of-home care during the day. Because of parental employment, up to 75% of our children are being cared for by someone other than their parents. Nationally, the majority of these children are receiving care in non-licensed facilities. Recent statistics in South Carolina show that approximately one-half of the children receive care in child care centers and half of the children receive care in family daycare homes.

This was shocking to me. So many children are receiving out-of home care, but is it the comprehensive, nurturing care that is so vital at this time of their lives? Is it just baby-sitting or is it providing the necessary tools for development? Remember, recent scientific data has shown that the majority of learning skills and personality traits are molded in the first five years of life. We aren't satisfied with babysitting for our school age and above children, and the time between birth and 5 years of age is just as critical (or even more critical) as the time after school entry. We should demand the best for our children during these early years of their lives.

Though physicians tend to focus on medical problems, social, educational, and socio-economic issues are equally important and need our attention. They are committed to addressing these issues, along with their colleagues. One of the ways that pediatricians work toward addressing these issues is the concept of the medical home, a team-based health-care delivery model led by a physician that provides comprehensive and continuous medical care to patients. Care in a medical home is defined as being <u>accessible</u>, <u>family centered</u>, <u>comprehensive</u>, <u>continuous</u>, <u>coordinated</u>, <u>compassionate</u>, and <u>culturally effective</u>. Medical care rendered with these principles in mind is therefore much more inclusive than just routine care, and addresses the more universal needs of our patients, families, and fellow citizens.

The Systems Approach

We recognize that the well-being of children and their families requires a truly multi-dimensional systems approach in which we guarantee healthcare (preventive care, routine care, and acute care), enhance education, minimize social inequities, address poverty, set legislative policy to minimize poverty and maximize education, etc. Each requires we become involved in a positive manner. Involvement is the key.

What's my point? Getting involved is crucial to creating positive change, which can only occur when we consider all aspects of the situation (all of the involved systems). Improvement in one system might be diminished if other systems are left unattended. Children are too vital for us to neglect any aspect of the support systems (family, education, socio-economic and others) responsible for their care. And yes, it really does take a village to raise a child. Even the most independent family relies on social resources for many aspects of life in modern society.

Each of us needs to look at the available systems for improving the health of children and devote some time and energy to making a difference. If the medical home should be *accessible, family centered, comprehensive, continuous*, coordinated, *compassionate, and culturally effective*, our approach toward others should be the same.

A commentary by an elected official in South Carolina referred to some of the less fortunate in our society in very unfortunate and pejorative terms. We cannot engage in rational discourse if we vilify, demonize, or dehumanize our fellow man. Whatever important points we wish to make, if we demean others, our discussion will not be heard—and deservedly so. The means (what we say and how we express ourselves) has an impact on the ends (what we hope to accomplish). To ignore that is to render oneself and one's message ineffective.

Involvement Beyond School—A Call

An address by Jonathan Franzen, author of the best seller *Freedom*, titled "Liking Is for Cowards. Go for What Hurts" was enlightening to me. The premise of his commencement address to Kenyon College was that it is far too easy in today's society to *not* get involved, especially with regard to love and commitment. He notes, "Our infatuation with technology provides an easy alternative to love." Technology allows us to connect with things and to "like" multiple things via various social media outlets. But those kinds of connections lack full engagement with our fellow man.

I particularly like one of his descriptions about love. "Love is about bottomless empathy, born out of the heart's revelation that another person is every bit as real as you are. And this is why love, as I understand it, is always specific. Trying to love all of humanity may be a worthy endeavor, but, in a funny way, it keeps the focus on the self, on the self's own moral or spiritual well-being. Whereas, to love a specific person, and to identify with his or her struggles and joys as if they were your own, you have to surrender some of yourself." He goes on to note, "To expose your whole self, not just the likable surface, and to have it rejected, can be catastrophically painful. The prospect of pain generally, the pain of loss, of breakup, of death, is what makes it so tempting to avoid love and stay safely in the world of liking."

Love for others requires involvement, both getting involved and staying involved. It requires our understanding of our common humanity and our willingness to accept one another on those terms. Mr. Franzen appropriately points out that there is a difference between liking and loving. We have to personally invest some of our emotional energy in our relationships and understand bottomless empathy before we can understand and can practice true love for others. That commitment to the specific individuals with whom we interact (investing our energies and showing a willingness to truly accept the inevitable pain that occurs in human relationships) underlies our ability to love each other. It is too easy to stay in the world of liking and to avoid the world of love.

The word empathy has had multiple negative connotations on the political scene. I personally don't see how anyone can be a bona fide public servant without having a heart full of empathy. If we can't see what other people see and we can't feel what other people feel, how can we pretend to act in their best interest?

Mr. Franzen concludes with the following, "The fundamental fact about all of us is that we're alive for a while, but will die before long. This fact is the real root cause of all our anger and pain and despair. And you can either run from this fact or, by way of love, you can embrace it. When you stay in your room and rage or sneer or shrug your shoulders, as I did for many years, the world and its problems are impossibly daunting. But when you go out and put yourself in real relation to real people...there's a very real danger that you might love some of them. And who knows what might happen to you then?" His call for involvement and commitment was and is a welcome additional reminder to me.

THE TAKE-HOME MESSAGE

Each of us has to commit to our loved ones and our fellow citizens with bottomless empathy. This allows us to engage and to be less inclined to disengage in our relationships with others. In the words of singer/songwriter Carole King, "You've got to get up every morning with a smile on your face and show the world all the love in your heart." That's how we help improve the lives of others and our community.

I hope people come here to this place to think about how they themselves can be better people rather than come here to reflect on death (parent)

(inscription from the wall of the Columbine Memorial)

Section 4
STAY INVOLVED

Chapter 29

Life-long Learning

How many times have we said, "Whew! School is over and I don't have to worry about reading or learning anymore!" We have all said it at the end of each school year or at graduation of high school or college. The implication is that learning only occurs in the classroom and only in the early stages of our lives. In point of fact, learning is a life-long task. Yes, life-long. We are always learning (or should be) how to improve our ability to work, to communicate with our families and friends, to socialize with our neighbors, and to enjoy life. We learn that there are many bumps along the way, but we can overcome them with determination and the help of our community.

Active, involved citizens are life-long learners and life-long mentors, people who recognize that learning is a combination of knowledge and experience. Knowledge (the acquisition of information and the logical application of that information) is always affected by life's experiences. And experience is always affected by one's knowledge—both are in a state of flux. Therefore, our lives are in an evolving equilibrium. It requires constant introspection to realize that we are, or should be, changing our responses to events and people over the years, based on new knowledge and experience. I'm convinced that we should never be content with only so much knowledge and experience. More knowledge enhances our experiences, and more experience enhances our knowledge base throughout our entire lives.

Our responsibility to our fellow citizens is to use this life-long knowledge and experience and become life-long mentors. The dictionary defines a mentor as "a trusted counselor or guide." We can be mentors for our children, our colleagues, our neighbors, and our friends. We can be mentors for almost anybody. As long as we maintain the proper humility and sincerity in these relationships, we can use our life-long learning to motivate, mobilize, mediate, and monitor issues in our community. None of us has all the answers, but working with and for each other, we can come up with the proper solutions to what might appear to be unsolvable problems.

The Process of Life-long Learning

How often do parents tell their children to stop doing something that they should not be doing? Often they are very puzzled and even discouraged. "I have told you so many times that you cannot do that. Why do you persist?" This is repeated in every household, probably every day. The learning process demands that parents understand that children don't always learn something the first time. They need constant reminders, and our job is to do that in a loving, caring manner. The learning process is just that—a <u>process</u>. Processes take time, and we need to remind ourselves of that constantly.

Teachers know this. Learning in the classroom is a process at each grade level and indeed over a student's entire primary and secondary education. Sometimes we actually have to learn things several times before it really sinks in and we understand what it means. In addition to teachers, people in many other professions know this: mechanics, doctors, plumbers, and electricians, to name a few. All of these folks know that things aren't learned the first time around. They and their consumers need frequent reminders. Remember, learning something doesn't guarantee that we actually understand. That takes time, energy, and commitment.

Conflict resolution is something that requires persistent instruction and learning throughout our lifetimes. And unfortunately it is not universally attained in our society. Some people seem to think that when they are grown they know all there is to know. Nothing could be further from the truth.

Children are taught by their parents and teachers how to deal with issues when things don't go right. Children need to learn that certain behaviors are acceptable and some behaviors are not. Since these issues always change, the learning curves for how to deal with conflict are always changing. Too many adolescents and adults assume that their work is done, when it never is. I have learned that I need to pay constant attention to this skill.

Adults not only have to learn how to successfully resolve conflicts, but they have to be models of such behavior. Far too often, especially in the realm of professional sports and politics and cable news, adults are the models of *behavior to avoid.* Any behavior that demeans, dehumanizes, or vilifies others is unacceptable. Any behavior that remotely encourages violence as a means of resolving conflict is not acceptable in a civilized society. If adults can't exhibit the right behavior, our children don't have a chance.

Learning how to resolve conflicts is a task we must undertake throughout our lifetimes. We need to stay involved throughout our lives learning how to deal with both good and bad things in life and to be good examples to our children and fellow citizens.

THE TAKE-HOME MESSAGE

Learning is life-long. We need to recognize this, continuing to participate in various initiatives and partnerships in our community. We must recognize that these initiatives and partnerships will change over time, and we will need to change and adapt also. Expect change to occur and prepare for it. Stay involved in the activities in our community, accepting change and actually participating in it. Stay involved by being willing to continue learning throughout your life. The most exciting lessons are always right around the corner, waiting to be learned.

Chapter 30

Necessary Traits for Staying Involved

Communities change through a slow steady process, offering brief glimpses of hopeful progress. Oftentimes the slow steady process seems unfruitful and the interval between the glimpses of progress seems like forever. Even the most motivated community activist can get discouraged. Yet we must be committed for the long haul. It is not easy. We cannot get discouraged, even when pessimists tell us that it cannot be done. We have to understand that our path to effective change may be very different than the one we envisioned.

Persistence and Optimism

Individuals who make a difference in the lives of their community embrace the opportunity to manifest personal change. They realize that to be effective agents of community improvement they must adapt to as circumstances shift. They allow the unexpected to reinvigorate their efforts toward positive change. Similarly, communities that make a difference by improving are the ones that embrace social change, as well.

For personal change and social change to occur, individuals and communities must be prepared to stay involved. Various community projects and activities might succeed, and we will be excited and enjoy our success. But it is equally likely that community projects and activities might have less than optimal outcomes. That is when our true resolve to make a difference shows up. That is when we must accept these less than satisfactory outcomes, roll up our sleeves, stay involved, and resolve how to improve the situation.

Some of you may say, "This sounds so pie-in-the-sky—folks will just give up when things don't go as planned." Well, I don't dispute that, but those who will truly make a difference will manifest two powerful attributes: persistence and optimism.

Persistence and optimism are essential traits to leading effective change. When we exhibit persistence and optimism, we don't get discouraged, even when pessimists tell us that it cannot be done. When we are persistent, we stay involved. We recognize that commitment to others is not intermittent. It is not off and on. When we persist in our efforts to improve our community, our involvement is continuous. We understand that the path to effective change may be a very different from what we planned. Our persistence must be heavily sprinkled with our ability to adapt and redirect our course as needed. Persistence means a willingness to continue to work with our neighbors to improve our community under all circumstances. Keeping that effort going when the projected outcome isn't necessarily good is particularly important. We must persist even when we might have to work harder. Persistence is needed if we are to make a difference in the community.

When we are optimistic, we accept that good things don't just happen because of us. We recognize that positive change is a group effort. When we are optimistic, we accept that bad things don't just happen because of other people. Less than desirable outcomes renew our efforts to improve our community. We don't complain—we move forward.

Tolerance

Many folks will recall the movie *Remember the Titans* as a football film. In my interpretation, this movie was about racial tolerance, and football was simply the vehicle to bring this story to light. Based on a true story that took place back in the early 1970s, it relives the experience of a high school in Virginia that was forced to integrate black athletes into their formerly all-white football team. In addition, the white football coach was forced to step aside and let the new black football coach lead the team. Tensions between students, athletes, parents, and coaches were obvious and, unfortunately, understandable. However, the athletes were able to learn that for the good of the team (and to win) they all had to work together as equals. It was not an easy lesson, and other students, parents, and coaches seemed to have an even more difficult time understanding this. Yet their ability to come together was what led to a successful football season and enhanced awareness of issues on both sides of the race barrier.

When it comes to improving racial relations, we are faced with the same dilemma. It seems at times that things are continuing to improve, and then we collectively take major steps backward, only to be subject to racially motivated brutalities. In the big picture, it seems as though change takes place in minuscule steps. The racial problems that we have had in the United States have dated back to the very beginning of this Republic, leading skeptics to say that we never really change. But I disagree. We are making change. Not as fast as I would like to see it happen, but it is occurring.

How can we ensure that positive change will continue to occur? We need to be tolerant and accept diversity. And remember that being tolerant and accepting diversity does not mean permitting behavior that offends or impinges on the freedoms of other people. We must remember that freedom is not an absolute right, but one that depends on all of us working together.

Compassion

Staying involved. That phrase reminds me of the hit disco song of the 70s, "Staying Alive." And, in many ways, the two of them are related. Staying involved in community affairs does indeed guarantee our staying alive, personally and socially. I recently received a letter from a mother who is staying alive. This mother has a genetic condition resulting in mild intellectual disability, and her three sons have the same condition with more significant disability. One of her sons is in jail. As I read her letter, I could sense this mother's total devotion to her children, her willingness to do anything that needed to be done to help her sons. Though she wonders why these things had happened, it didn't keep her from rolling up her sleeves to help her children. This mother was not content to simply get involved in the lives of her grown children despite her own problems. She wanted to *stay* involved.

A recent church service also reminded me of our need to stay involved. The Presbyterian Church (USA) includes the following in its Declaration of Faith: "In its concern for justice in the social order, God has never forgotten the needs of individuals. In the end, the Lord will judge all persons by the simple, unremembered acts of kindness they did or failed to do for the least of their sisters and brothers. We believe that God sends us to risk our own peace and comfort in compassion for our neighbors. We are to give to them and to receive from them, accepting everyone that we meet as a person; to be sensitive to those that suffer in mind or body; in ways that confirm dignity and responsibility. We must not limit our compassion to those we judge deserving."

Our compassion for others is what allows us to get involved, stay involved, and do the right things for others. This includes our friends and our enemies, those deserving and seemingly undeserving, those with good fortune and those who are less fortunate. By doing the right things for any of these people, we are doing the right things for everyone.

Patience and Commitment

Individuals with patience will accept good times and bad times in stride and keep going by staying involved. They keep their emotions balanced, getting excited when good things are happening and using that energy to continue to improve the community. They don't get overly exuberant during good times. They also don't get discouraged when they are faced with difficult issues or tough times. Yet they don't take all the credit for the positive results. They realize it's a team effort. They are willing to stay with the effort and to work together with others in the community. They have patience, and continue to work hard for their community. Though life and its changes can be a real roller coaster, folks with patience keep an even temperament and keep going.

Working toward positive change in our community requires our personal commitment to the problems in the community and our realization that these problems are our problems. If we accept the problems in our community as our own problems, we are committed to seek solutions that can make a difference. We accept the personal responsibility for issues in our community and become committed to tangible solutions.

Empathy

It's easy to get involved in the community, especially with a pet project. These projects keep our interest as we try to make a difference. But we have to be ready to accept new direction at times, since times change, interests change, and relationships change. And levels of enthusiasm (or personal energy) definitely change! Sometimes these changes make it easy to stay involved, but oftentimes these changes make it more difficult to stay involved. So what's the key to sustained involvement? Well, I think it is empathy.

Empathy is the trait that allows us to put ourselves in someone else's shoes to understand their situation and their responses to it. Empathy is also one of the most difficult personality traits to employ on a regular basis. In Section 6 I discuss the ongoing struggle each of us has with the practice of forgiveness. Well, the practice of empathy requires similar effort because it is difficult to be empathetic as often as we should be. We easily lose our focus and our ability to maintain our empathy as changes are occurring all around us. But to make a tangible difference in our efforts to improve our community, empathy needs to remain at the forefront. How else can we respond to the continued needs of our community and our fellow citizens?

I try to remind myself of the words of Leland Kaiser, whom I first mentioned in Section One when I tend to lose my focus—I am the problem, I am the solution, I am the resource. Those twelve words serve to remind me that through empathy I share in my community's problems and I share in in responsibility for seeking solutions. How else does empathy keep us going in our community?

- Empathy reminds us that we are all in this together,
- Empathy reminds us that the actions of others cannot necessarily be judged by us,
- Empathy reminds us that, rather than judge others, we should make tangible strides in improving the life of our community and the lives of our fellow citizens,
- Empathy reminds us that we are responsible to a Greater Being than ourselves, and ultimately we are here to serve others, and
- Empathy reminds us that the world doesn't revolve around us, that we are just a small part, but capable of significant good.

THE TAKE-HOME MESSAGE

The traits of persistence, optimism, patience, tolerance, compassion, patience, commitment and empathy guide us in our community improvement duties, staying involved in our quest to help each other and our community.

Chapter 31

Sage-ing—An Additional Perspective

As we age, an anniversary can be a delightful experience. The remembrance of a wedding ceremony or the birth of a loved one or a celebrated day in our history conjures up happy thoughts, yet rarely moves us to significant action to improve our community. The remembrance of the death of a loved one or a catastrophic event such as September 11th, 2001 evokes sad thoughts, but sometimes moves us to make a difference. Events in 1999 in Littleton, Colorado at Columbine High School reminded me of the ever-fragile balance in society between positive and negative influences. The young men in Littleton performed an isolated act of violence, but they lived in a culture that tends to accept intolerance and has difficulty resolving conflict.

The challenge with getting involved in our community is staying involved. No matter what you get involved with, things will change. We all want positive changes to occur. Yet we are all uncomfortable with change because it means we have to change also. It is difficult to stay involved with community activities when things evolve or change differently than we had envisioned. We shouldn't accept change just because change is inevitable, but we do need to be willing to adapt.

Sometimes it is easy to get involved in projects in the community, but to make a <u>real</u> difference we need to stay involved. Sages stay involved. They demonstrate the following:

- Commitment. It takes a significant effort to be committed to make a change in our community. Sustained effort demonstrates that commitment;
- Ownership. If we take ownership or personal responsibility for issues in our community, we become involved and stay involved because improvement means something to us. Difficult issues that we often avoid (such as teenage pregnancy or drugs) are now ours to deal with and to actively assist our fellow citizens;
- Investment. When we stay involved in our community, we are making an investment, a personal investment, in our community. And the exciting thing is that this investment is similar to a financial investment. With the proper investment of time and energy, there can be a substantial return on the investment. The result can be greater than our individual contribution;
- Asset-based community building. When we get involved in our community, we tend to look at difficult issues in a different light. We tend to look at our strengths or assets and try to build on those strengths instead of just complaining about problems. I think it is fine to recognize problems, but only if we are willing to contribute in a positive way to correcting these issues;
- Interaction. By staying involved in our community, we meet and interact with some amazing people—our fellow citizens. These interactions can be remarkably satisfying as we work together for our common good; and
- Positive action. When we are involved, we are not passive. We are active participants. We aren't sitting on the sidelines, waiting for someone else to do the work. We can take personal and community satisfaction in the positive changes that occur from our active participation.

How to avoid becoming a curmudgeon

I once gave a talk for a Sunday school class and was asked how to avoid becoming a crotchety old man or a curmudgeon (a bad-tempered, difficult, cantankerous person). Initially I was stumped by that question, but I now think the proper answer is gracefully accepting change *and* being part of the process.

No matter what you become involved with, things will change. Yet we are all uncomfortable with change because it means we have to change also. We shouldn't accept change just because change is inevitable, but we do need to be willing to adapt.

Brief Literary Example

Many years ago I read a delightful, little book by Mitch Albom entitled *The Five People You Meet in Heaven*. Mitch dedicates the book to his uncle who he states, "gave me my first concept of heaven." The main character in the book, Eddie, led a relatively simple life. He was the son of a very hard working family that struggled for everything they had. Eddie was a World War II veteran and suffered physical and emotional scars from the turmoil's of war. He returned home and married his sweetheart, yet was unable to pursue his life's dreams because he had to assist his father. He worked as a maintenance man at a local amusement park. He died saving a child from a damaged ride at the park.

What are the lessons of the book?

- Connectivity. We are all connected to one another. You cannot easily separate one life from another. All our lives intersect. One action of one person can have a profound effect on another without the original person even knowing it.
- Sacrifice. "Sacrifice is a part of life. It's supposed to be. It's not something to regret. It's something to aspire to. Little sacrifices. Big sacrifices. A mother works so her son can go to school. A daughter moves home to take care of her sick father...sometimes

when you sacrifice something precious; you're not really losing it. You're just passing it on to someone else."

- Hatred and forgiveness. The hatred that we sometimes feel toward individuals because of significant wrong-doing has no benefit in our lives. It is critical that we learn to accept the frailties of ourselves and of our fellow human beings, exercise forgiveness and move on.

I'm sure other important lessons can be extracted from this short book. As Mr. Albom states, "everyone has an idea of heaven, as do most religions, and they should all be respected. The version represented here is only a guess, a wish, in some ways, that my uncle, and others like him—people who felt unimportant here on earth—realize, finally, how they much they mattered and how they were loved."

Every life in our community matters. As we work together to improve our community, we need to exercise total personal commitment to improving the lives of everyone. Commitment is a life-long journey to stay involved in the health of our community. Quiet individuals such as Eddie in *The Five People You Meet In Heaven* are just as committed and involved in improving our community as more vocal members of the community such as government leaders or op-ed writers such as me. These quiet committed individuals live good lives each day, providing excellent role models for us all.

THE TAKE-HOME MESSAGE

The community improvement process involves all of us for all of our lives. We are all connected, and we need to work together. Every little act to improve our lives can have a dramatic impact in the long run. We need to use the experience of aging to become sages in our communities.

Chapter 32

Involvement through Tough Times

Parenthood is one of those times when we must want to get involved and stay involved in the lives of children as emphasized in Section 2 and Chapter 26. And we have no choice—we have to get involved. We have previously mentioned that parenting is the toughest job in our lifetimes, and I guess that one of the significant reasons for its difficulty is the need for constant involvement from parents during tough times.

Adolescence

We all become discouraged, for good reason, when we see children and adolescents who do not have parents involved in their lives. A recent article in a pediatric journal addressed the issues of parental monitoring and its association with adolescent risk behaviors. The investigators looked at various adolescent risk factors—sexually transmitted diseases, sexual behaviors, marijuana use, alcohol use, antisocial behavior, and violence. The group of adolescents was asked if their parents knew where they were or who they were with most of the time. For those adolescents with less perceived parental monitoring ("they don't know where I am or who I am with"), the results are not surprising. That group was more likely to be exposed to sexually transmitted diseases or engage in risky sexual behavior, marijuana use, alcohol use, antisocial behavior, or violence., These findings are probably predictable to many readers. But the message is clear. Parental involvement in the lives of our children is critical to their development and safety

Adolescence is a particularly difficult period for children and parents alike. Teenagers are in the process of developing into young adults with self-autonomy. Yet it is our never-ending duty as parents to protect them from harmful and dangerous behaviors that affect them and others. We cannot (and should not) be constantly in their face" as they grow older and assume more responsibilities; but we must know what's happening in their lives, monitoring, and intervening when appropriate. We want to help correct deficiencies and praise their successes. (Let's not forget this latter point.)

Divorce

Divorce is an unfortunate and frequent occurrence in our society. Since it affects all of us (divorced or not), we need to be able to deal with the consequences of divorce. We also need to be able to see how it affects our communities and what we can do to make a difference. A recent medical article notes that 1.5 million children are affected each year in the United States by divorce, and these children are more prone to mental health problems, lower academic achievement, and higher levels of drug use than children of non-divorced parents. This study demonstrated the need for and effects of long-term prevention strategies for children of divorce. How do these prevention strategies come about? Through parental involvement! By staying actively involved in the lives of the children, divorced parents can still make a positive difference.

The study was undertaken to demonstrate the long-term effects of such intervention; short-term benefits had been previously demonstrated. Over 200 families with adolescents were studied. Two intervention programs involving the adolescents and their mothers (the mother program and the mother-child program) were used. These programs employed active counseling (more than 20 hours) for the mothers alone in the first program and for the mothers and adolescents in the second program. Positive results were noted at a six-year follow-up. Both of the intervention programs worked. The adolescents (males and females) had significantly reduced symptoms or diagnosis of mental disorders, decreased marijuana, alcohol, or other drug use, and decreased number of sexual partners. This latter statistic is particularly significant, since fewer partners decreases the risk of teenage pregnancy and premature sick infants.

Both of these programs focused on improving mother-child relationships, father-child relationships, effective discipline, effective coping, and reducing negative personal thoughts for the children of divorce. What is the bottom line about all of these issues? It should be no surprise any more: getting involved with our children and staying involved through stressful times is the key. By staying involved, we can deal with even these tough issues and, working toward better self-esteem and coping skills for our children who are at increased risk for a variety of problems.

THE TAKE-HOME MESSAGE

The involvement of divorced parents is an absolute necessity in the lives of our children. The responsibility never ends, just the degree of monitoring changes over the years. We don't let our younger children run out into the street, so we shouldn't let our older children engage in equally life-threatening behaviors (for example, exposure to AIDS or drunk driving). Involved divorced parents can improve the chances that their children will have fewer mental health problems, less drug use, and decreased risk of teenage pregnancy. Know your children, know where they are, know what they are doing, and know whom they are with.

Chapter 33

The Everyday Lessons of Genocide

My parents, in their early adult years, were exposed to the horrific revelations of the Holocaust—the unimaginable slaughter of six million Jews and others, men, women and children. The world community vowed to make sure that would never happen again. Yet, such tragedies have continued—Rwanda, Kosovo, Darfur. History shows that the tragedies of genocide have existed since the beginning of mankind.

In a civilized world, one would innocently ask, *How can this happen?* How can we let these things happen? What is wrong with us? How can good people allow the evil doings of a twisted few people?

I think the lessons of genocide throughout history teach us that we do have some responsibilities in this matter and that we cannot just blame others for unspeakable things that were done. We contribute to some of the underlying culture that allows discontent and hatred to brew. We need to change that culture.

The following are lessons of genocide, caveats that are no less pertinent today. They strongly suggest that we:

- Be aware of unproven media hype—propaganda can be our own worst enemy;
- Never dehumanize others—it's far too easy to paint with a broad brush, identifying others as less worthy than we, or say that an entire group deserves indictment because a small number of people commit heinous crimes. Close to 1 million Rwandans were slaughtered in a

very short period of time in 1994, and Jews were rounded up and sent to concentration camps and gas chambers during World War II as a result of such dehumanization. I think this is perhaps the most serious breeding ground for genocide. I have heard so many disparaging things about Russians during the Cold War and Muslims during the Gulf Wars, peoples spoken about as if they were subhuman. Yet the overwhelming majority of these folks are not evil. In that sense, we contribute to the underlying culture that breeds hatred;

- Treat everyone as we would treat our own family;
- See how one person can make a difference: Paul Rusesabagina in Rwanda (in the movie *Hotel Rwanda*), and Oskar Schindler in WWII (in the movie *Schindler's List*). Both of these men chose to do the right thing, although it was life-threatening.
- See that, though one person can make a difference, we need the help of a team to accomplish significant work; and
- Reach out to others and solicit their assistance. We should never be shy about asking for help to do what is right.

As I was reviewing the lessons of genocide recently, I realized that these are the same lessons to be learned for staying involved in the area of community improvement. We can never work together to help each other unless we adhere to the points mentioned above. The lessons of man's inhumanity toward others should help us realize our own humanity and the need to work together to improve our lives and the lives of our fellow citizens.

THE TAKE-HOME MESSAGE

Genocide occurs <u>because</u> we assume things without finding out the truth, <u>because</u> we view other people as less than human, <u>because</u> we don't treat everyone as we would our own family, <u>because</u> we don't realize that one person can truly make a difference, <u>because</u> people don't work together as they should, and <u>because</u> we don't ask for help as often as we should.

Chapter 34

Captain Miller to Private Ryan: "Earn This"

One night, when I was channel-surfing, I found myself at the end of the movie, *Saving Private Ryan*. Every time I watch that film, I am deeply moved by the final sequence of events.

As the army captain, Captain Miller (portrayed by Tom Hanks), is dying on the bridge, he leans over to Private Ryan (portrayed by Matt Damon) and whispers in a dying gasp—"Earn this." I must admit it took me a while to really understand the full magnitude of this death-bed request. He means that multiple lives were lost in an effort to find Private Ryan and to bring him home to a family that had already lost their other sons in the war. He means that Private Ryan needs to honor his fallen comrades with a life of service toward others. He also means "earn this" in a much broader sense. Freedom is not free. We all have a responsibility to have an active role in our community. Thousands of soldiers died in World War II to save us from the tyranny of despotic regimes. He is saying that it is our responsibility as well as the responsibility of Private Ryan to live a life from this point forward to earn this sacrifice.

Private Ryan stands over the body of Captain Miller, And then we see him as a mature adult paying homage to Captain Miller's gravestone at the Normandy battleground cemetery. He is there with his wife, his children, and his grandchildren. Private Ryan asks his wife if he has led a good life, and I think by extension asks himself if he has "earned this" life. He is asking himself, "Did I honor Captain Miller and all of my fallen comrades by leading a life that helped others and contributed to my society?"

"Did I earn this?" is the burning question in his mind.

Now what's my point here? This movie and its ending are a poignant reminder of the responsibilities our freedoms entail and the absolute necessity of all of us to remain involved in our communities throughout our lifetimes. Only by staying involved can we be positive contributors and understand how we have to work together to make a difference. Much like life after the tragedy of 9/11, the ultimate way to respect those who lost their lives for our freedom is to live lives of community involvement with an understanding of our collective responsibility to each other.

THE TAKE-HOME MESSAGE

Our lives are not really our own. We are here for a purpose that is greater than we realize. We must stay involved to help foster a greater good. We must earn the sacrifice of those who died for our freedom. Our job is never done.

Chapter 35

Martin Luther King, Jr.'s Dream

Perpetual dreaming is a way to stay involved. I use the term dream to mean a strongly desired goal or purpose or something that fully satisfies a wish. We all have dreams about how we feel society can improve itself and how societies can live in peace. At the same time, reality usually fractures those dreams and renders us so skeptical that we don't think that it can happen. I disagree. If we can dream about being on the moon and put a man on the moon, we can accomplish our dreams. If we can dream about unraveling the DNA code of genetics and unravel such a code, we can accomplish our dreams. I am a firm believer that if God gave us the ability to unravel the complexities of the physical sciences, we have also been made capable of solving the seemingly impossible problems of social life. We have to dream the solutions, and then do the work. Social problems are no less solvable than the problems of physical science.

On August 28, 1963, one of our truly great Americans said, *"I still have a dream. It is a dream deeply rooted in the American dream. I have a dream that one day this nation will rise up and live out the true meaning of its creed. We hold these truths to be self-evident, that all men are created equal...I have a dream that every valley shall be engulfed, every hill shall be exalted and every mountain shall be made low, the rough places shall be made plains and the crooked places shall be made straight and the glory of the Lord shall be revealed and all flesh shall see it together...With this faith we will be able to work together, to pray together, to struggle together, to go to jail together, to climb up for freedom together, knowing that we will be free one day...When we let freedom ring, when we let it ring from every tene-ment and every hamlet, from every state and every city, we will be able to speed up that day when all of God's children, black men and white men, Jews and Gentiles, Protestants and Catholics, will be able to join hands and sing in the words of the old spiritual, 'Free at last, free at last, thank God Almighty, we are free at last'."*

Martin Luther King, Jr. sacrificed his life for this dream. From the early days of the Montgomery bus boycott until his death in Memphis, Tennessee, he lived his undying devotion to this dream.

We can all learn from Rev. King, who had no use for inaction even when he was jailed. We must stay continually involved in the activities of our community. Dreamers get involved and they stay involved for positive change to occur.

THE TAKE-HOME MESSAGE

I hope that I stay a dreamer for the rest of my life. Dreaming is one sure way to make a difference.

My friend was laughing and then it turned into crying and I thought, my God, why is this happening to us. (student)

(inscription from the wall of the Columbine Memorial)

Section 5
LOVE FOR OTHERS

Chapter 36

The Gift of Love

There is no greater gift from God than love. We all think we know love. We listen to love songs. We read books or watch movies about love. We write love letters (or love e-mails). But there would not be all of the intolerance and hatred present in our society if true love prevailed. But how do we define it?

We define love more by actions than by words.

Let me give an example. Many years ago, I was moved by a sermon that reminded me about the need to care for (to love) everybody, but especially those less fortunate or downtrodden. In that sermon, Jill Johnson-Duffield (Associate Pastor, Greenwood First Presbyterian Church) noted that there is an unbreakable link between faith and love. She eloquently stated, "We will not be able to persist in humble reliance on God's grace, even in the face of silence, unless we first recognize our need for mercy and are moved to demonstrate that mercy to others...When the needy, hated stranger comes yelling at us for mercy we will turn away unless we understand, know in our heart, that we are the very stranger, too...What seems like a hindrance may take us precisely where God wants us to be involved."

Very powerful words. Yet to love others as the Pastor described has proven immensely difficult for our society to do on a collective basis.

But what would our world be like if we could? Just as the love of God represents the light shining out of the darkness, our love for others will make each of us shine and illuminate the glory of our maker even more. We can change our community one neighborhood at a time by the daily expression of our love for each other, to accept the grace of God and pass it on. It is the ultimate act of kindness.

Deeds

Another particularly enlightening sermon entitled "Does It Matter What I Do?" (drawn from scripture in the First Book of Corinthians) tells us that all of our positive acts toward others *do matter*. Reverend David Mayo reminded us that our works or deeds serve to glorify a higher calling, not solely for our benefit. They are done to benefit others, that's why these acts matter. Small acts of kindness —that smile, that handshake, that door opening, that thank you, that nod in traffic— all serve to demonstrate our love for others.

There should be no disputing that these small acts turn into larger acts of kindness. When we are doing positive things, we are also much less likely to exhibit intolerance that poisons relationships.

Acts of kindness toward others should reflect our empathy: the fact that we can put ourselves into someone else's place and see how they should be treated; the fact that we can see their situation and respond to their needs; and the fact that we can see the need for social change and agree to be a part of it. This latter type of empathy, social empathy, requires a lot of work, because we usually have built-in biases that have developed over years or decades of living. Yet social empathy is just as important as personal empathy. We don't make progress in social change and community improvement by saying words. We make progress by our deeds. All of our positive deeds benefit our fellow citizens and put us on the road toward community improvement.

Incredible sacrifices have been made on our behalf in the past. Countless American soldiers have lost their lives so that we could have the opportunity to improve our lives. We cannot forget our heritage. We cannot forget their sacrifice. We must always strive to exhibit love for others, recognizing that we are never finished. There is always one more act of kindness we can do. It is these acts of kindness that will eventually make the difference in our lives.

Intolerance

Hatred and intolerance appear to be more prevalent in our society and our world than they should be. Innocent civilians die daily in the Middle East turmoil. Law enforcement officers are shot in the line of duty. Citizens being arrested are sometimes subjected to unnecessary abuse. One of the most horrific scenes recently is the equivalent of a mob lynching in Chicago of two men whose van seriously injured some pedestrians. Instead of attending to the injured pedestrians, the mob dragged the driver and the passenger from the van and brutally murdered them. We could cite numerous incidents that unfortunately occur daily. At times, we seem to be numbed to these events and their consequences unless they affect us personally.

The dictionary defines intolerance as being "unwilling to grant or share social, political, or professional rights; unwilling to grant equal freedom of expression." I think it is the same unwillingness that sets up these incidents. Some of these acts defy explanation and some are irrational acts performed by people who are seriously disturbed. But many of these acts represent the culture or the environment that we live in. What do I mean? If we are intolerant of others (often expressing our disdain as hatred toward others or their actions), we teach our children that it is ok to fly off the handle without considering the consequences of those actions. Reasoned, calm understanding must be used, especially when we think it necessary to judge other people and their actions.

Don't get me wrong. I am not saying that people are not accountable for their misdeeds. They are. But we are just as likely to make mistakes. Let's be careful about judging others, especially when we avoid the beam in our own eyes.

Often our society has condoned irrational or senseless responses to certain common situations as "OK." Just look at sporting events, where rude or derogatory remarks are often the norm for players and fans, and are actually accepted (and even expected!). Emotions run high at sporting events, but sportsmanship should also be expected all the time. Too many children learn trash talking and physical intimidation through the examples of their elders.

Intolerance is moving backward, not forward; we have lost our empathy, which is our moral rudder, so we flounder, adrift in a sea of hatred. It requires many steps forward and a great deal of time to overcome intolerance's negative influence. It's so much easier to be cognizant of our actions, ensuring they advance relationships, not hinder them. We need to remember that what we do matters.

Barriers of technology

Our ability to exhibit love for others is tested everyday, and if we are honest, we will admit that we have plenty of room for improvement. Why? One reason might be that it is easier to be impatient and intolerant in today's society than to be calm and accepting of the good in others and in the events around us. Modern society and our technology-based methods of interaction enforce impatience and intolerance. "After all, we ought to be able to get what we want, whenever we want it. Right?" Well, that is not the way life is, yet we are constantly trying to replace relationship-building with new and more advanced technology, hoping to make life better.

I am in favor of technology, but not at the expense of the interpersonal acts and deeds of love for others at their very core. Interpersonal relationships work to build healthy families and households. Interpersonal relationships work to build healthy neighborhoods. Interpersonal relationships work to build healthy communities.

Music as a Beacon

I have had the good fortune to see Ken Medema perform. Ken's music tends to be loud and this sometimes offends sensitive churchgoers. However, Ken's music is loud more in message than volume. His words pack a powerful punch. Although Ken is blind you would never guess that from the powerful visual imagery in his songs.

In his CD, *In the Dragon's Jaws*, Ken notes that "On this little planet, wracked by war, cultural decimation, environmental degradation, and fear, faith people are called to work, dream, plant, risk, love, sing and dance." He emphasizes that "There is always hope, where it seemed there was no hope to be had." He suggests that we make a habit of filling our days with the following acts and deeds in order to show love for others:

- Work – nothing is accomplished without hard work
- Dream – dare to do something you've considered impossible
- Plant – sow seeds for tomorrow's generations
- Risk – don't be afraid to step out on a limb for others
- Love – accept the grace of God and pass it on
- Sing – loud and clear
- Dance – with joy!

Similarly, the Broadway musical and movie *Rent* starts with the musical number "Seasons of Love." The song highlights the fact that there are 525,600 minutes in a year. With unbelievable beauty in words and music, the song drives home the point that each of those minutes is an opportunity to fill our lives and our community with love. We can look back and reflect over a week, a month, or a year and try to determine what we have accomplished or need to improve, but the song tells me that I should consider smaller time frames. I should seek to use every minute to exhibit love for others, and that means doing the right things for my family and my fellow humans. Every minute offers a new opportunity to make a difference – a new season of love.

Folk singer/songwriter David Roth also has a poignant song titled "Before I Die." In the song, he states, "Before I die I want to be the richest man in history." But his definition of riches is "a wealth of friends [and] abundant love that never ends." What a cool description of riches! To measure one's wealth in friendships and abundant love is indeed a wonderful measure of life.

If we tie the latter two songs together, the message is clear—in every minute of the day (525,600 in a year), we have the opportunity to develop friendships, nurture friendships, help others, improve our lives, and improve our community. These opportunities can make us exceedingly wealthy, if we try.

THE TAKE-HOME MESSAGE

Love for others exhibited through positive deeds and exhibited through overcoming intolerance can help our fellow citizens and the life of our community. What we do does matter, and it matters all day, every day.

Chapter 37

Features of Love
Trust

Trust is one of the outward manifestations of love for others. If you trust someone to do the right thing and they trust you to do the right thing because they see trustworthiness in you, your relationship thrives. Equally exciting, the two of you can work together to help bring about positive change.

But trust seems to be hard to find in our often-cynical society. Webster defines the noun *trust* as "assured reliance on the character, ability, strength, or truth of someone or something." The verb *trust* means "to commit or place in one's care or keeping, to rely on the truthfulness or accuracy of." Boy, both of those definitions are tough to follow. And we should not confuse gullibility (getting duped or cheated) with trust.

As a physician, I hope I have proven trustworthy over the years to families who place their trust in my decisions about their health care. Sometimes it's easier to trust professionals to do the right thing and very difficult to trust our fellow citizens (or citizen groups) to do the right thing. Yet it is the latter form of trust (citizen to citizen, citizen-group to citizen-group) that must occur if we are going to make positive changes in our communities. Professionals or governmental officials cannot make positive change happen until we can trust our fellow neighbors and citizens enough to work together. This is a two-step process—we must trust each other and then do the necessary work to improve our communities. Robert Putnam, author of *Bowling Alone*, has reported enhanced life expectancy in more trustful communities. What a positive side effect!

Faith

It's easy to talk about love for others. We can come up with many examples to demonstrate it: helping our neighbors, donating to charities, working in a soup kitchen, or working at a homeless shelter, to name only a few. It's tough to find the time and energy, mental and physical, to do many of the tasks that require commitment and willingness to do the work.

I think the toughest part of displaying love for others is to have faith in your fellow citizens. Yes, the ability to exhibit love for others requires the faith to see the intrinsic value in others; the faith to believe that others, given the right opportunity, can make the right choices and be productive citizens; and the faith that we can do this together. This same faith should be extended to our children.

The ability to listen to peoples' concerns and to offer a fair and balanced response is based on our ability to trust each other. And this trust depends on faith in others, the same faith that God has in us.

Now, I don't mean blind faith. People are fallible and make mistakes. We should not put others or ourselves in danger by assuming that everything will be just fine. We need to be cognizant of the frailties of others, but not to the point of being cynical about everyone. When we are cynical or doubt the intrinsic worth of others, we cannot also be trusting. Such cynicism destroys our ability to work together to improve our lives and the life of our community.

Gratitude and Mercy

There should be no question about the necessity of love for others; this concept seems intuitively obvious, something that should be easy and straightforward. But often our intolerance of others interrupts our ability to truly exhibit love. In addressing two of the critical elements in love, I need to thank Harold Kushner and an unknown psalmist.

Harold Kushner, bestselling author of *When Bad Things Happen to Good People* and *Living a Life That Matters*, penned another book about the healing wisdom of the 23rd Psalm. This book, *The Lord is My Shepherd,* is a wonderful analysis of some of the most beloved lines in the Bible. Rabbi Kushner spends an entire chapter on each line, providing a thoroughly insightful interpretation to help all of us understand this psalm anew. His interpretation helps us understand why we seek solace and comfort in the psalm at times of distress, usually at the loss of a loved one. Two lines in particular, "My Cup Runneth Over" and "Surely Goodness and Mercy Shall Follow Me All the Days of My Life," emphasize two of the critical elements of love for others. Those elements are gratitude and mercy.

"My Cup Runneth Over" acknowledges gratitude for the ever-present blessings of life. Kushner reminds us that "Gratitude is rooted in the sense that life is a gift...that comes to you from someone else, not by your own efforts...and as such it is a physical representation of the love and caring the giver feels toward you." He further notes that "Gratitude is a reciprocal process, giving and receiving at the same time." Our lives are therefore "an accumulation of gifts that God has given us" and once we are able to realize that, we now know that our cup does truly runneth over. Since gratitude is a reciprocal process, Kushner suggests that once we appreciate the gifts that have been given to us, it makes perfect sense to extend the same gifts to others.

"Surely Goodness and Mercy Shall Follow Me All the Days of My Life" offers the great good news that we don't have to achieve goodness and mercy. They follow us if we let them. Goodness means feeling good about life and oneself, and mercy means the discovery of forgiveness in the world. Kushner points out that mercy can mean loving kindness or unearned love, poignantly reminding us that mercy "asks us to do things for others that we don't have to do and that the other party might not deserve, but we should do them anyway." Since we are extended unearned love or mercy from God because of His love for us, we must extend this mercy toward others.

Appreciation of Others

As I was driving one day, the music and lyrics from a movie, *Disney's Pocahontas*, wafted out of the car speakers. I found myself singing along and I realized that a significant message was right there for me. The movie provides a delightful, yet ironically sad, look back into the intrusion of English settlements into the lands of Native Americans. I enjoyed the movie with my son many years ago and had forgotten the joy (and sorrow) of its message. The song "Colors of the Wind" provides a reminder of the need to be aware of all that is around us. We need to appreciate everything, and we need to manage it respectfully so it reaches its full potential.

Three stanzas stand out as prime examples:

> *You think the only people who are people/Are the people who look and think like you/ But if you walk the footsteps of a stranger/You'll learn things you never knew you never knew.*

This stanza serves to remind us of our tendency to view the world solely through our perspective. As we learn to accept the differences in others as attributes to be nurtured and cherished, we will be able to "learn things we never knew we never knew."

> *The rainstorm and the river are my brothers/The heron and the otter are my friends/And we are all connected to each other/In a circle, in a hoop that never ends.*

The metaphors in this stanza, referring to animals and nature, by logical extension also refer to our fellow humans with whom we are fully connected always.

> *For whether we are white or copper skinned/We need to sing with all the voices of the mountains/We need to paint with all the colors of the wind.*

This stanza refers to the differences between the white settlers and the Native Americans, but by extension we can use these lyrics to remind us about our external differences that exist, yet do not preclude our commonality. We need to listen to and see the "voices of the mountains" and the "colors of the wind" as we work together. One might argue that these voices and colors refer directly to nature and its beauty and our need to protect those things, and I would agree. Yet I also see the "voices of the mountains" and the "colors of the wind" as elements in the song of life that can guide us as we advance the cause of love for others by working to improve our communities at all times.

THE TAKE-HOME MESSAGE

We need to employ every available sense, to be keenly aware of what is going on around us. Only then can we appreciate the complexity and the interrelatedness of our community. Only then can we work together (with trust, faith, gratitude, and mercy) for a common good, exhibiting love for others by our awareness of issues in the community and our willingness to work toward solutions to our common problems.

Chapter 38

President Lincoln's Message

In a society where the motto is "In God We Trust," love for others should be relatively easy to come by. Yet we know that nothing could be further from the truth. We have a tough time with this one. Sometimes it's relatively easy to love certain people, but tough to love other people. If we're going to make a difference in our community, though, we have to be willing to work with everyone. Hatred toward one group or another would never allow a community to advance and improve itself and the lives of its citizens. We have to be willing to love one another as we work toward a common goal.

During the Civil War our country was ripped apart at the seams, brother against brother, family against family, countryman against countryman. Over 620,000 Americans were killed, more than in any other conflict our nation has ever experienced. Yet as the conflict was winding down, our government and its people were faced with the daunting task of rebuilding the country and re-forging the ties of love and friendship. Abraham Lincoln, in his 1865 Second Inaugural Address, realized this difficulty and offered the following conciliatory remarks in his final paragraph.

> *With malice toward none; with charity for all; with firmness in the right, as God gives us to see the right, let us strive on to finish the work we are in; to bind up the nation's wounds; take care for him who shall have borne the battle,*

and for his widow, and for his orphan – to do all which may achieve and cherish a just, and a lasting peace, among ourselves, and with all nations.

Despite the bloodshed and the hatred, Lincoln knew the only way to rebuild and move forward was to accept common responsibility for the problems of the day, *with malice toward none* and work together to improve from this time forward, *with charity for all*. These words and thoughts ring true today.

THE TAKE-HOME MESSAGE

Love for others leads to an acceptance of the commonality of goals and purposes, our common humanity. Love for others is the only way to effectively improve our community and, ultimately, ourselves.

Chapter 39

Freedom and Sacrifice

"I can do whatever I want to. It is a free country. Don't tell me what I can't do!" We seem to live in a society where these phrases are accepted without proper reflection. There are too many irresponsible actions performed under the guise of personal freedom. We do indeed do live in a free country, yet we are not free to do whatever we choose. The privilege of freedom is tied to the responsibility of freedom. This was very well stated in an editorial in the *Atlanta Journal-Constitution* in 1996 titled, "A Plea for the Common Man."

> Since its founding more than 200 years ago, America has celebrated the merits of the common man. Rejecting a European tradition that governing was a right reserved to the propertied rich, the American experiment was founded on the notion that all men were created equal and that a person could not be measured by the size of their bank account ... as a nation, we have begun to accept the notion of "opting out" of public programs in favor of more private individual approaches. America threatens to become a country in which the well-off professional class is sealed away from the rest of the nation by walled communities, private security, and separate schools and health care systems... In the long run, attempting to opt out of social challenges cannot work and the cheap security promised by that approach cannot last. Problems such as ignorance, disease, crime, and social

unrest cannot be quarantined into one area or economic class. They do not respect boundaries or walls or wealth. That is the deeper meaning of Thomas Jefferson's phrase, " All men are created equal." We are all in this together, as Americans.

When our exercise of personal choice wrongfully affects other people, we irresponsibly use our freedom. You see, our freedom is not really ours. It is a gift, and we must use that gift wisely. Great sacrifices have been made on our behalf. And we must honor those sacrifices. We can do most of the things that we want to do, but we cannot do everything. The laws of physics tell us that for every action there is a reaction. The same principles apply to social interactions. For everything we do, we must consider the consequences of those deeds and make sure we are using our free choices responsibly. We must always answer to others and God.

I'm learning that it's never too late to learn more about freedom and responsibility, that's one reason why I must confess that I'm enjoying the aging process! I'm enjoying using my over half a century of experience and, at the same time, learning new things all the time. The combination of experience and life-long learning allows for us to adapt to, and accept, change. Contributing constructively to change is one of the major challenges of adulthood.

The other exciting thing about aging is learning about perspective, learning how my life relates to the sacrifices of those from previous and current generations. Thousands of soldiers and civilians have sacrificed their lives so that my family and I can live in freedom. This has become a sobering realization for me.

Growing up in the 1960s and coming of age in the Vietnam War era, I now know that I did not have a good understanding of personal sacrifice and the critical importance of teamwork, and I welcome the opportunity to continue learning about these principles. Three decades in medicine has also helped me with this. I now know that any activity worth doing requires a significant group of people working together and willing to sacrifice for the good of the whole. After all, we are a country based on a government of the people, by the people, and for the people. If you observe and practice these ideals, you exhibit love for others in all your actions.

THE TAKE-HOME MESSAGE

Life is a constant blending of learning, experience, and change. Freedom is not an absolute right. We must behave in a proper and responsible manner in all of our actions. I have learned that the sacrifice of countless others represents their ultimate expression of love for the rest of us. We need to do everything we can do to honor their legacy.

Chapter 40

Humbled by Goodness
Nicolai's story

One day, as I was driving home and listening to public radio, I heard an absolutely remarkable story. It was about Nicolai Calabria, a 13-year-old boy from Massachusetts who climbed Mount Kilimanjaro in Africa to raise money to provide over 1,000 wheelchairs for people in Tanzania. That might not sound amazing, but Nicolai was born without a right leg and had to use crutches for the climb.

The story starts back when Nicolai saw a documentary called *Emmanuel's Gift*, about a man from Ghana who endured a similar hardship and accomplished a significant physical feat to raise money for the less fortunate in his country. Like Nicolai, this young man also had a severe right leg birth deformity that made his feat even more remarkable pedaling one-legged on a bike to raise awareness about the plight of disabled children and adults in Ghana. The movie moved Nicolai to consider how he could make a difference by raising money for the Free Wheelchair Mission. This organization uses lawn chairs that can be fortified and have wheels added. For just $45 each, these wheelchairs can be sent to people who desperately need them in impoverished countries.

Nicolai's father is a climber, so the two of them decided to train together. This is not an easy climb. Mount Kilimanjaro is more than 19,000 feet above sea level, and the ascent is about 13,000 feet from base to summit. The climb took over five days to finish. High altitude sickness is a significant potential complication, and both Nicolai and his father suffered from it. Headaches, shortness of breath, and dizziness are symptoms of high altitude sickness. Nicolai's father became so ill that he had to stop just 140 meters from the top. Nicolai continued on to the top, accompanied by guides, at his father's urging.

His original goal for fundraising was $25,000 and at the time of the radio broadcast he had raised over $53,000. His efforts will make it possible for over 1,000 wheelchairs to be gifted to the people in Tanzania. Someone inspired Nicolai, and now his story is an inspiration to all of us.

Acts of Kindness

Folks often talk about random acts of kindness. I like to think that acts of kindness do not have to be random. I would like to think that such acts are the norm, not just randomly distributed amongst our interactions.

When people talk about random acts of kindness, I presume them to mean the following:

- Acts of kindness done without any obvious reason.
- Acts of kindness done without knowing the person the act was directed to.
- Acts of kindness done without knowing that these acts will be acknowledged.
- Acts of kindness done without a motive other than love for others.

When people refer to such acts, the implication is that they are few and far between. But using the definitions that I mentioned above, these acts are some of the most important and meaningful things we can do, the acts performed just because it was the right thing to do. These are the actions of people often times unheralded at the time that they occur, but that leave a lasting impression on their beneficiaries. We can all think back to times when somebody did something that we couldn't believe and the impact that had on us, hopefully changing our own patterns of behavior.

I'm reminded of such acts when I drive around town later in the spring, such a gorgeous time of year in the South, when we're past the suffocating layers of pine pollen, and the trees are full of greenery. Yards everywhere are festively decorated, following our annual ritual of planting a variety of bedding plants in pots, planters, and small areas in the yard. Many yards have such small areas for plants that one might wonder why folks would even take the time and effort to plant flowers.

Well, I know. Because they're beautiful. Because they lift up our spirits. Because they are the perfect symbol of our renewed energy. Because they symbolize our renewed efforts to beautify our community and to work to improve our community. I'd like to think that these seemingly minor efforts at beautification, these spring flowers, can take on an even greater significance. These flowers can remind us that the beauty of nature should spark us to do what we can, wherever we can to improve the lives of others and our community. The beauty of flowers should remind us that selfishness has no place in social interactions. Flowers bloom not because of us but because of a higher power that has created them. We are not in charge of this process.

We should also be reminded that flowers can be planted, but without the proper nutrients and water, they will wither and die. Community relationships also need nurturing by random acts of kindness.

THE TAKE-HOME MESSAGE

Our lives should be persistent efforts to improve the lives of others. Nicolai's quest and acts of kindness are a true celebration of a significant effort in that direction. They are the symbolic flowers that beautify our society. Yet their real beauty is in their lack of selfishness. These acts are done for others because it is the right thing to do.

Chapter 41

Communal Responsibility

*C*ommunity development. *Community improvement*. What do these terms mean? I'm sure they mean different things to different people. To businessmen and businesswomen they probably mean community growth and more business opportunities. For teachers, they might mean enhanced opportunities or programs for their students. For health professionals, community development and community improvement might represent things other people take care of while they concentrate on health matters. For citizens, they represent programs or processes that other people set up on their behalf. In other words, I don't think we have a clear idea about what it means to engage in community development or community improvement.

To improve the life of our community, we need to exhibit love for others. It seems to be one of the most obvious things to do to improve life in the community. Yet it is actually one of the toughest. Because it means we have to acknowledge that we are all equal in God's eyes.

What does that mean, to be equal in God's eyes? We need to be willing to roll up our sleeves and help everybody, not just our friends. We need to help those who we don't necessarily like (our enemies), those who we might consider undeserving, those who we don't feel comfortable around, and those who are less fortunate. Why? Because we are all equal. None of us is any better than anybody else. We accept the grace of God for our imperfections. We need to pass the grace of God on to others and know that they have similar imperfections.

If we can accept the grace of God and be forgiven, why do we find it so hard to extend the same to others? We need to learn to accept the mistakes of others. We often rationalize our inability to help others by stating that we "didn't like them anyway" or that they are "not deserving." We shouldn't do that.

THE TAKE-HOME MESSAGE

To truly make a difference in our community, we need to downplay our personal agendas and personal definitions for community development and improvement and accept a communal responsibility to improve community problems such as bullying (see Chapter 5). We need to protect those that are victimized. We have to learn that we are all equal, that we all need help in our lifetimes, and that we all need to help each other. Love for others demands that we maximize good influences on our children and minimize bad influences on our children.

Chapter 42

People of Love: A Variety of Examples

One of the things that I have emphasized over the years as I wrote about the Five Steps is that all of the steps are important. Yet I must admit that the act or acts of exhibiting love for others probably ranks at the top. The love we show via our words and actions provide the fuel for all of our other actions as we attempt to be good parents, to get involved, to stay involved, and to practice forgiveness. While we strive to do the right thing, it is always a worthy exercise to look for examples to remind us of how to lead our lives.

But first, an important reminder that nobody is perfect. The people mentioned below and others honored for their service to others all have flaws that do not negate their positive actions, but serve to remind us that we can always improve. We should try to emulate the good deeds of others, but not devalue those good deeds because of some flaws in the individuals who performed them.

William Wallace

The life of William Wallace was the subject of the movie *Braveheart*. In that movie, he led his fellow Scottish countrymen to rebel against the tyranny of the English rulers. When asked why he was willing to die for the cause, he replied "Every man dies, not every man really lives." My interpretation of that quote is that one of the most important things in life is to do the right thing. Doing the right thing can often make us uncomfortable or can be threatening. But doing the right thing is "really living" before we succumb to our inevitable death.

Atticus Finch

Harper Lee's novel *To Kill a Mockingbird* chronicles a white lawyer defending a wrongly accused black man in the days of significant segregation and racial intolerance. Why would a prominent lawyer in a small southern town risk his friendships and social standing to defend what many of his neighbors considered a second-class citizen? As he told his daughter, he did it so he could live with himself. He knew he had to do the right thing, no matter what others said.

Rosa Parks

Ms. Parks finally decided to sit down on that bus in Montgomery, Alabama in the early 1950's instead of yielding it to a white person because she knew that she was no less a person than anybody else. The color of her skin did not make her inferior. It was the right thing to do and by taking a stand she helped her fellow citizens start the process of standing up for their rights.

Jean Valjean

Victor Hugo's novel and the Broadway musical, *Les Miserables*, follows the life of a man, Jean Valjean, punished for stealing a loaf of bread to feed a starving child. After he was released from prison, he eventually was able to start a successful new life. He used his success to help care for the less fortunate, making choices that often put his own well-being in jeopardy. By doing the right thing and loving his fellow man through actions, he was able to realize a peace in his life not previously known.

Franz Jägerstätter

In 1943, in the heat of World War II, Franz Jägerstätter, at the age of 36, was executed for his refusal to serve in the army of the Third Reich in Germany. As a youth and young adult, he had quite a reputation for being wild, then married, settled down and served in his parish church. He devoted himself to his faith and sought solutions to problems through that faith, recognizing that he was unable to reconcile himself with the participation in the atrocities of Hitler's regime that was required of him, and that his conscience left him only one option: his steadfast refusal to serve.

Franz was willing to sacrifice himself for the common good, serving as a rare example of defiance in the face of the evil of a social movement gone wrong. One might argue that his singular act did nothing to stem the tide of the Nazi regime. I argue that his commitment to his God, and by extension to others, will serve as a perpetual example of one's ability to rise above the current situation and do what is right. He left his wife without a husband and left his children without a father. His eldest daughter was not quite six when he was beheaded for treason. Yet it appears that God had a greater plan for Franz Jägerstätter, and he accepted that, having already overcome his early troubles (gang violence, temporary banishment from his village, and fathering a child out of wedlock) to turn his life around through his devotion to his faith. It is of interest that he is now being reviewed for possible sainthood by the Catholic Church, one proof of the importance of his actions and what they demonstrate to the rest of us.

We are called to sacrifice for others. Fortunately, we rarely have to sacrifice to the level of Franz Jägerstätter. The idea of sacrifice at any level is still difficult for most of us, even though the relatively modest sacrifices we are called upon to make are merely to accept appropriate change and appropriate compromise. We need to adapt to change to help others, and we must be able to compromise. For the latter, we have to accept the reality that our view of a given situation is probably not the only right view.

Martin Luther King, Jr.

The election of 2008 was a moving experience for me. My mother always taught me that true equality of opportunity was our constant goal, though it had not yet occurred in her lifetime. So many images flashed before my mind during the celebration in Chicago, when Barack Obama gave his acceptance speech for the Presidency. I saw Eisenhower's use of federal troops in Little Rock to desegregate Central High School, George Wallace's defiance, James Meredith's enrollment at the University of Mississippi, the Selma, Alabama marches and Bull Connor's water hoses, the assassination of John F. Kennedy, the assassination of Robert F. Kennedy, the assassination of Martin Luther King, Jr., the riots in the Watts section of Los Angeles, the Rodney King riots, to name a few. The hopes and dreams of so many people were realized with the election of Barack Obama as our next President.

Now I realize that not all were pleased with the outcome of the Presidential election, yet I hope that all can realize the significance of this outcome and its relationship to a remarkable individual who dreamed it.

Martin Luther King, Jr. delivered his famous "I Have a Dream" speech in front of the Lincoln Memorial (see Chapter 35). His words excite me every time I read them. They remind me of my responsibilities to others and the need to keep moving forward. As Abraham Lincoln reminded us in his second inaugural address, we should act "with malice toward none; with charity for all."

Bui Doi

The musical *Miss Saigon* is a haunting reminder of the horrors of war and the social conflicts off the battlefield that adversely affect so many people. One of the most heart-rending songs from *Miss Saigon* is called "Bui Doi," referring to the children left behind after war, the American-Asian children fathered by American soldiers, the children often nobody wants. The term *Bui Doi* is Vietnamese for "the dust of life." The brief lyrics to this ballad are as follows:

> They're called *Bui Doi*
> The Dust of Life,
> Conceived in Hell
> And born in strife.
> They are the living reminders of

all the good we failed to do
We can't forget
We must not forget
That they are all
Our children too.

Unfortunately, all wars leave such scars on society, and not always by illegitimacy. Children suffer from the innocent death of siblings and parents in war. Even smart bombs cannot prevent the inevitable loss of innocent lives. Whether those lives are in New York City (World Trade Center), Iraq, Palestine, Israel, Sudan or Rwanda, children suffer from armed conflict and indeed are "the living reminders of all the good we failed to do."

THE TAKE-HOME MESSAGE

The physical expression of love for others is the willingness and fortitude to do the right thing, taking care of the less fortunate, our children, and our elders. Sometimes it's easy but often times it's really difficult. But by doing the right thing, we can really live and make a difference. Remember, "Every man dies. Not every man really lives."

Chapter 43

Children in Foster Care

I recently attended a leadership conference of the American Academy of Pediatrics in Chicago. One of the featured presentations was a talk by Francine Cournos, MD. She is a psychiatrist who, as a child, endured the loss of both parents by age 11. Though she had assumed that her aunts or uncles would take over as guardians for her and her siblings, they did not. So at age 13, she was placed in foster care until she moved out on her own at age 19.

She described some of the humiliating processes that she had to endure in foster care. First, she had to be "processed" – going from one office to another, from one stranger to another, as different information about her was collected. Then she had to get a physical examination from a local physician. This step was particularly humiliating, being examined in an unfamiliar environment by a stranger. Finally, she had to meet her new foster parents. Since this placement was not permanent, she and her siblings had recurrent cycles of attachment and desertion.

In her book, *City of One, A Memoir*, she notes the various mental states that she went through. On the surface, she acted like a miniature adult, "but underneath...was a very needy child who suffered from depression, self-hatred, distrust of adults, an inability to make any intimate connections, and a tremendous loss of a sense of structure. In short, I was not what I appeared to be." Dr. Cournos knows (from personal experience) that children placed in foster care might not articulate their needs as adults do, but "they watch, worry, observe the behavior of the adults around them, perceive that they are being left out or underestimated, [and] contain their feelings they judge too dangerous to express.

"[Foster children] pass judgment, censor their speech, feel powerless and powerful at once. They take responsibility for, and feel guilty about, developments in their lives that are in fact out of their control. They invent theories to explain what is happening to them, and believe that whatever happened before, however unlikely it may have been, is bound to happen again." Finally she realizes that "it is unrealistic to believe that children who have had no solid grounding in the first place can suddenly become capable adults simply because they have reached the legal age of eighteen."

Dr. Cournos beautifully and dramatically articulates the trials and tribulations of this era in her life. I was profoundly affected by her account. At the meeting in Chicago I heard other presentations about the plight of children who end up in foster care because of a variety of family disruptions. I now realize that more children are in foster care than I appreciated. These children have special healthcare needs, both physical and psychological. These needs have not been adequately addressed by our society, especially some governmental policies, state and federal, that often short-change the services needed by these children and their families. The magnitude of the foster care problem is substantial.

THE TAKE-HOME MESSAGE

We need to provide extra support and services to a particularly vulnerable group of children, foster children. These children require our special attention in order to become productive citizens. They need our help to become adults who learn how to "be nice" and to help others. By learning the important lessons of caring, loving, sharing and helping, all of our children will exercise true love for others and have a greater likelihood of being happy.

Chapter 44

Loving and Liking

Some time ago, I was handed a copy of a sermon delivered in Greenville, SC and published in the *Greenville News*. The article was titled "Working with the People We Don't Like," by Ludwig Weaver. Pastor Weaver starts out his discussion about two individuals who appear to be very dissimilar on the surface. One graduated from Clemson University, the other graduated from the University of South Carolina. One was a staunch Republican, the other a staunch Democrat. They seemed to be polar opposites, yet they attended the same church. Much to their chagrin, their minister asked them to be co-chairs for a church capital campaign fund. How could these two work together?

This brief example was a great lead-in for the rest of the article, where one of the questions asked is "How do we work with people we don't like?" To be successful at this, there are some key elements that need to be remembered, according to Pastor Weaver.

- We need to remember that we are all sinners. This means that we are all fallible. We all possess faults and all of us will irritate someone.
- The Bible demands that we love all people. That means that we work for their good and that we do all that we can to help them. We acknowledge them as children of God and wish the best for them.

- The Bible does not demand that we like everyone, especially if they do or say unkind things. But we can still work for their good; that is, exhibiting love for others through our words and deeds.
- When it comes to a group of individuals who say or do unkind things, we must remember that God created them and that God loves them as He loves us. The constant reminder of our own sinfulness should dampen our harsh evaluation of others.
- We must remember that the grace of God extended toward us is also extended toward others, unconditionally.

The principles above also hold for relationships within our families. We might be very upset and not like the words or actions of our family members, but that should not diminish our love. As a matter of fact, the strength of our love should allow us to work to create positive examples and, hopefully, future harmony in family relationships. As I have previously mentioned, parents often have to say or do things that their children do not like. Parents must continue to be parents and be positive examples for their children, yet recognizing their own potential fallibility. This delicate balance is what makes life a continuous journey for all of us.

THE TAKE-HOME MESSAGE

It is oftentimes very difficult to work with people we don't like, especially if we consider their words and actions hurtful. We must learn how to handle our own reactions to these people, yet keeping the higher goal in mind—unremitting love for others. Maintaining a balance between not liking the words and actions of certain people, while professing our love for all, is a difficult one. Thank God for giving us the ability to maintain this balance as we work toward improving the lives of others and the life of our community.

Chapter 45

Sportsmanship

I am a rabid sports fan. I love to go to sporting events, and I love to watch them on TV the same way I listened to them avidly on the radio as a child. This habit, unfortunately, takes away from otherwise productive reading time, so I have to self-impose certain limits.

Sports play a significant role in society. They emphasize the need for fitness and exercise, sorely lacking in our society as a whole. Sports remind us of the interactive role of mind and body, and that physical conditioning and technical expertise will not triumph without the right mental attitude. As a matter of fact, sometimes the right mental conditioning will allow folks to prevail over their physically superior competitors. Sports are also a social experience for so many of us as we cheer together for our common goal, the success of our teams. We collectively share in the victories and defeats and often have a collective pride in our team's accomplishments.

Yet, the world of sports today is often the very symbol of what is wrong in our society. Sports talk shows make it their business to belittle people under the guise of journalism. Taunting on the football field (for example "sack" dances) are excused as showmanship or the business of sports entertainment. Tennis certainly has had its bad boys with their inane antics that probably boosted ratings. Players often dance around as if they are the best player in the land after a remarkable win, forgetting that they had an even greater number of failed moves. I could go on and on with many more examples.

So what's wrong with these displays? Such boasting or intimidation tends to breed an atmosphere of intolerance that pervades our society. What they primarily display is a shocking lack of sportsmanship.

Webster's dictionary defines the embodiment of sportsmanship as a player "who is fair, generous, a good loser, and a gracious winner." I think there has been a general deterioration in sportsmanship, blamed in part by media attention to the poorest sportsmen and their equally unsportsman-like fans.

Yet I think true sportsmanship is one key to our beginning to make positive strides toward improving our community. Sportsmanship exemplifies the right attitude toward others—fairness and generosity—which are loving attitudes. If we are good losers and gracious winners, we are showing love for others.

The sporting arena is one of the primary places for us to demonstrate that we can engage in spirited competition without losing sight of the fact that life holds a bigger purpose than just winning or losing. That purpose is to help others and to help our community be the best they can be. The lessons of true sportsmanship are truly the lessons of life, if we only listen. These are hard lessons to learn but the ones with the greatest impact. If we learn fairness, generosity, the ability to both win and lose gracefully, we will have learned how to deal fairly, generously, good naturedly and graciously with our fellow citizens.

THE TAKE-HOME MESSAGE

The example of sportsmanship sets the stage for positive community improvement. Sportsmanship demonstrates love for others, respect, and honesty, and graphically illustrates the right way to deal with our fellow citizens. Let's always be fair, generous, good-natured and gracious, no matter the playing field.

Chapter 46

Contemplation

As I found myself listening to folk music recently, I realized that I was listening to some of the formative music of my youth. Well, graying hair, aching joints, and living through the death of one's parents makes me reflect on my life to consider where I've been, where I am, and where I still need to go. The contemplative strains of folk music certainly allow for such reflection

Singer/songwriter David Roth issued a CD titled *Rising in Love*. Each of the songs offers a unique perspective and speaks clearly to the need to embrace others. I highlight three of these songs:

- "The Armor Song" talks about a stoic father advising his son to always protect himself in interactions with others by hiding behind a "shield" to avoid being emotionally vulnerable. His mother advises him to the contrary saying that only by "letting your armor down" will you truly be a man. With the revelation of his mother's wisdom, he now knows that when he becomes a parent, he won't let foolish pride get in the way. He will "wash him [his child] up with laughter, rinse him off with tears and fill him up with loving that"ll last him all his years." I just love that latter description that directs us to instill the care and love of our children with a sense of vitality ("laughter") and sensitivity ("tears"). Hopefully, they will do the same for their children.

- "Legacy" deals with an aging father, a daughter undergoing a career change and a son (Mr. Roth himself), each contemplating their legacies. I wouldn't be able to state it better than the songwriter, as he notes "Here's to every aging person and all those in their prime and to passing on the love that you receive, for wisdom, grace and kindness and the power of that love will be the measure of the legacy you leave." Again, wow! Wisdom, grace and kindness doled out to others via our love will be our legacy. What a great way to be remembered!

- Finally, the song "Manuel Garcia" relates the true story of a young adult who has terminal cancer. The effects of the disease and the treatment leave him weak, thin, and bald. When his wife and friends come to take him home from the hospital, they arrive with shaved heads to lighten the moment. When he arrives home that same day, the whole neighborhood (over fifty strong) has shaved heads and a "We love you" banner. The song ends with the following, as said by Manuel Garcia– "I felt so alone with my baldness and cancer; now you stand beside me; thank Heaven above, for giving me strength that I need. May God bless you and long may we live with the meaning of love." By sharing in his baldness, everyone was ready to emphasize how much they loved Manuel Garcia and were willing to help him through very difficult times in a truly unique and effective way.

THE TAKE-HOME MESSAGE

Love for others can be demonstrated in so many ways, and it is absolutely crucial that we do so if we hope to improve our community. We need to take time to contemplate ways each of us can work together to make a difference. My thanks to David Roth (see also Chapter 36) for leading me to take time to pause and reflect.

Chapter 47

You've Got a Friend in Me

My youngest son and I decided to celebrate a recent Father's Day by attending *Toy Story 3*. He has grown up with Woody and Buzz Lightyear, and we spent many hours playing Toy Story and watching the movies, to the point of memorization. When he was younger, we watched the movie for the pure enjoyment of the fantastic talking toys and the comedy of their interactions. Now that he is older (and I guess I am too) we still watch the movie for the fantasy and the comedy, as well as with a sense of wonder at the creativity of the *Toy Story* creators. We appreciate anew the movie's message, as well. What do I mean by the message? Let me explain.

An op-ed piece in the *New York Times* by David Hajdu ("The Toys Are Us," June 20, 2010) discussed the allegory, or moral fable, that *Toy Story* represents. The toys can be viewed in several ways: the toys that are relegated to the toy box after years of play perhaps represent the "graying of the American population," *and* they can represent the "idealized conception of our moms and dads as selfless, wholly subservient providers of unconditional love."

First, our aging population should never have to live without our devotion and love. They might lose some of their physical abilities, but they are still capable of guiding us in many ways by being our mentors, our mediators, our monitors, our mobilizers, and our motivators. Love for others, especially those aging, should be just as undying, as our love for our favorite toys. I'm not equating toys with people, but noting that the movie serves to remind us that change will occur, and just as we outgrow our toys, we will need to adapt to the changes in our relationships as the years pass by.

Second, Mr. Hajdu notes that Woody and Buzz seem to represent the idealized view of moms and dads. All of us who are parents and have aging parents know that parents have multiple issues that they must face as they get older. They continue to be parents with undying love for their children, but they have to adapt to the changes that aging throws at them. Just as their focus naturally adapts to their situation, so must we make appropriate accommodations to ours.

I will not reveal the ending of the movie, other than to note that beautiful "change" occurs. If we use the fable of *Toy Story 3* as an example, the children found a way to renew their love for their aging elders and parents. I was enthralled!

The original song written and performed by Randy Newman is titled "You've got a Friend in Me." What a fantastic message, that through good times and bad times we can always support each other, truly exhibiting love for others. As an excerpt from the song says, *"You've got troubles; well I've got them too. There isn't anything I wouldn't do for you. We stick together and we see it through. You've got a friend in me."*

THE TAKE-HOME MESSAGE

Love for others might be seen as a process that, though intuitively obvious, always needs to be rejuvenated. Change occurs, and we must change as well, to make sure that when the time comes we can adapt, never failing to care for our increasing aging population and parents, and welcoming their experience as well.

I no longer take anything for granted.
(student)

(inscription from the wall of the Columbine Memorial)

Section 6

FORGIVENESS

Chapter 48

An Essential Trait

Forgiveness is essential to human existence. The ability to forgive allows us to move on in our lives, progressing from childhood to adolescence to adulthood. Forgiveness is therefore a fundamental developmental step in our lives, without which, we could not make progress.

Indeed, more often than not, it's the inability to forgive that leads to hatred and intolerance in our society. Without the ability to forgive, we cannot grow as individuals, sharing life's pleasures with our family, our friends, and our community. We are all human beings. We are not perfect. We will make mistakes. We are accountable for our mistakes, and we need to take responsibility for them. Yet, the next step after recognizing mistakes and assuming responsibility for our mistakes is forgiveness.

A modern day bestselling book touches on this very topic, *Tuesdays with Morrie*, by Mitch Albom, details the philosophical ideals of Morrie Schwartz, a dying college sociology professor. Morrie asked the author (and us, the readers) some very simple, yet profound, questions about life:

"Have you found someone to share your heart with?"
"Are you giving to your community?"
"Are you at peace with yourself?"
"Are you trying to be as human as you can be?"

If we are truthful with ourselves, we will admit that we have made mistakes. But Morrie goes on to remind us about forgiveness, a relatively simple, yet devilishly difficult process. "Forgive yourself. Forgive others. Don't wait." stated the kindly gentleman dying of a progressive disease of the nervous system. "I mourn my dwindling time, but I cherish the chance it gives me to make things right."

That is a very powerful series of thoughts. We must forgive ourselves for our indiscretions and mistakes (accepting responsibility and apologizing) before we can go to the next level. Then we must forgive others who might have wronged us. And we cannot wait. Morrie tells us, rightly, that we cannot go on with our lives unless we do those three things.

Most of the time, we do hurtful things to people not knowing what we have done. Only after time has passed and we have gained experience can we realize that we have been wrong. If we eventually realize the error of our ways, why are we so hesitant to apologize? Why are churches so slow to apologize for past errors? Why are governmental bodies and politicians so slow to apologize for (or even recognize!) past errors? Why are we as citizens, neighbors, family members, spouses, and parents so slow to apologize for past errors? Is it pride, concern about possible loss of authority, obstinacy, or unwillingness to compromise? Well, it is all of those things. Our humanity gets in our way, and often keeps us from doing the right thing, reinforced by that fact that conflict resolution is poorly taught and slowly learned in our lifetimes.

"Forgive them, Father, for they know not what they have done." The words of Jesus Christ are as valid today as they were two millennia ago. The ability to forgive is the most difficult trait to execute and exhibit on a regular basis. Yet the message of Jesus Christ's crucifixion and resurrection cannot be clearer—we must learn to recognize our own mistakes and forgive ourselves. We must learn to accept the mistakes of others, practicing forgiveness. Only then can we learn to love others and learn how to work together for our common good.

THE TAKE-HOME MESSAGE

How can we apply all of this to community activities? Expect mistakes, accept responsibility, forgive ourselves, forgive others, and do it now! Abraham Lincoln told us that our democracy was a government "of the people, by the people, and for the people." We are all in this together. Differences and disagreements can lead to tangible change if we can exercise our opinions calmly, accepting responsibility, and practicing forgiveness.

Chapter 49

Components of Forgiveness
Vulnerability

W hy is it so very hard to forgive others and ourselves? I think vulnerability is the key. Nobody likes to be vulnerable, since it is perceived as a position of weakness. To be vulnerable, according to the dictionary, means to be "open to attack and damage," and to truly forgive someone and to accept forgiveness from someone, we must be vulnerable, to be not in a position of power but of equality, which can make us uncomfortable. We must accept that we are no better than anybody else.

Our culture tends to discourage this manner of conflict resolution, preferring the hotheaded approach. Calm, rational discourse seems to be discouraged. Just watch our legislative bodies, federal and state, if you need to be convinced. To be calm, deliberative, and willing to forgive means to accept the possibility of vulnerability. Now this doesn't mean we should not prevent ourselves from receiving possible emotional or physical injury. I think it means that we have to be vulnerable enough to be sincere and humble before those we are seeking forgiveness from, or those seeking forgiveness from us.

It's a constant struggle, but the most important struggle of our lives. By the grace of God, we are forgiven. We can do no less for others.

Sincerity and Humility

Two significant characteristics, sincerity and humility, are hallmarks of people who practice forgiveness. The dictionary defines sincerity as honesty of the mind, or freedom from hypocrisy. People who are sincere are genuine in their feelings and express earnest devotion without reservation or misgiving. This, perhaps, is one of the more difficult components of forgiveness. It is very difficult for us to swallow our pride and genuinely express regret for our own actions, and to forgive others for their perceived hurtful actions.

However, without sincerity, forgiveness is hollow. Sincerity demands honesty and openness in our apologies for our misdeeds. That stance will gain us acceptance. If we are insincere, however, our apology is seen as incomplete and often perceived as being worse than no apology at all. We must be genuine and honest when we issue or accept an apology.

The dictionary also defines humility, another important ingredient when it comes to forgiveness, as the state of not being arrogant or assertive, but reflecting or expressing a spirit of deference. Our pride often gets in the way of our ability to let humility govern our actions by taking us a revealing step back and looking at the situation, recognizing our humanity and the humanity of others. We all make mistakes. These mistakes, at times, hurt ourselves and hurt others. When we practice humility so that we can respond to these issues without escalating aggression, we have taken a giant step in the right direction. Sincerity and humility are traits that need to be integrated into the lives of our children so that they learn how to handle conflicts in an effective way.

Reconciliation

I wish I understood forgiveness better. This is a bit of a confession. I wish I were better at being able to forgive. I'm pretty good at it on Sunday after church, but I need to constantly remind myself during the week to practice forgiveness. I wish it just came naturally, but I have to really try hard at times.

Life is not perfect. There are plenty of circumstances when we get upset. One could argue that anger and hatred are undesirable innate responses to certain problems. Hundreds of years ago, such behavior might have been helpful for survival, but, more often than not, in today's civilized society these behaviors are destructive and counter-productive.

When it comes to our relationships with others, sometimes words don't help, as they can often be inadequate or misinterpreted. Often actions don't lead us in the right direction, either. As we contemplate our responses to various situations, we often find it difficult to understand what we should do. I, for one, find myself in this quandary frequently. I might be able to know in my mind what I consider to be right, but still have doubt about what I should do. Then, even if I solve my mental dilemmas, I have to resolve to do what I think is right, and this can be really tough. This type of exercise (trying to decide what is right and then acting accordingly) happens every time we face the issues of forgiveness, the most difficult task in our lifetimes.

During the last half century of my life, I have been evolving through various stages of forgiveness. I'd like to think that I'm pretty savvy at this point and can recognize the need to forgive myself for my own failings and others for their transgressions. This process is called reconciliation. I still have trouble with forgiveness for one of the most important relationships in my life—my father. His less-than-honorable behavior at many times (secondary, in part, to alcoholism) left many scars in my family. He has been dead for close to 25 years, and I should be able to come to grips with this, exercising forgiveness and moving on.

An additional component to my dilemma is the Fifth Commandment: Honor your father and mother. How do I honor somebody whose behavior was less than honorable on multiple occasions? Fortunately, a pastor of the Brunswick Church in Troy, New York, Harry Heintz, has addressed these issues in an article in the *Presbyterian Outlook*. Pastor Heintz suggests the following ways to honor parents:

- Accept their imperfections and limitations. They know that they are not perfect. We do not have to repeat their mistakes, but we are bound to, if we deny them.
- Forgive them for their shortcomings. Parents need forgiveness, even if they are too stubborn to ask for it. Some of us may have

dead parents we have never forgiven. Let God know that you forgive them.

- Live well, loving God first, not fulfilling their [parents'] expectations for our lives, but God's expectations for our lives. To become our own persons—better, to become God's persons—is to honor our parents.

I now realize that I need to resolve these internal conflicts and move beyond them. Pastor Heintz notes that some parents were abusive, some substance abusers, some unfaithful, and some absent. "To honor such parents is not to tolerate their abuses, but to move beyond them and become honorable people by God's grace."

Susceptibility

When we practice forgiveness, we are susceptible to significant feelings and sensitivities, both ours and those of the individuals around us. Sometimes the inability to deal with our feelings and provide the appropriate sensitivity to others impedes our ability to be susceptible to the changes needed to practice forgiveness. The susceptibility associated with forgiveness is good and worthy of our humble consideration.

No one likes to appear wishy-washy and always gushing with emotion. That's not what's being asked for when we practice forgiveness. If we are sincere in exercising forgiveness and humble in our approach, then we will find ourselves appropriately vulnerable and susceptible to our emotions.

The Problem With Politics

Politics is so difficult because politicians usually refuse to accept the vulnerability and susceptibility that are necessary for the practice of forgiveness. By adopting the necessary posture for forgiveness, they feel that they are seen as weak and ineffective. I argue that they are seen as quite the contrary! By appropriately exercising forgiveness with sincerity and humility whenever it is appropriate, our leaders would exercise more Christian principles and better serve their constituents. Leaders should always consider their journey in leadership no different than their life's journey—filled with life-changing experiences that require flexibility and adaptability. We also need to add in the qualities of empathy, open communication, and the acceptance of change, qualities necessary for effective debating and policy decision-making.

THE TAKE-HOME MESSAGE

I don't think that I can sum up this article any more effectively than to close with the refrain from the beloved hymn "Here I Am Lord". To practice forgiveness, we need to accept our common humanity and our vulnerability with sincerity and humility, be ready for reconciliation, be susceptible enough to accept change, and then declare – *Here I am Lord/ It is I Lord/I have heard You calling in the night/I will go Lord/If You lead me/I will hold Your people in my heart.*

Chapter 50

A Life-long Process

We all start out as babes and progress to toddlers, children, adolescents, and adults. At each step, significant developmental progress must occur to enable us to advance to the next level of personal and social growth. Along the way, in a nurturing environment, we learn to accept love from others and to express that love in return. Along the way, we also learn that people make mistakes. It is natural to get upset when these mistakes affect us personally, but if we do not learn how to forgive and move on to the next level, we get stuck in our developmental progress. Learning how to forgive is not something that occurs just once in your life. It occurs at every step along life's pathways—infancy, toddlerhood, childhood, adolescence, and adulthood. It also occurs almost daily at each of those steps.

The ability of a five-year-old to forgive is very different from a fifty-five year old. However, we all know people who often seem to be stuck at the five-year-old level, not able to accept that we are all fallible. I think that more emphasis needs to be placed on the ability to forgive in the learning process through schools and the ability to master this process through adulthood. Morrie Schwartz was embarrassed to admit, in his final days, how his inability to forgive a close friend led to the collapse of a friendship—and for all the wrong reasons. How often have we done similar things?

Many tasks in life can be mastered after some hard work and then are easy to continue. Tasks such as riding a bike, programming a DVR, using a remote control, or driving a car. Forgiveness is not such a task. We learn to practice forgiveness as children, as adolescents, as young adults, as mature adults, and as senior citizens. Our ability to accept and extend forgiveness depends on our level of maturity at the various life stages. Yet, just because we can do it one day doesn't mean we can do it the next day. Each time can be just as difficult (or even more difficult) than the last time.

Each time we are wronged or do something wrong, there are emotional issues that need to be solved before we can move on to forgiveness. Dealing with these emotional issues with sincerity and humility is the backbone of learning to practice forgiveness. Because these emotional issues can be so difficult, we have a lot of soul searching every time something goes wrong. Practicing forgiveness is like learning how to ride a bike anew every time. We have to learn how to pedal and balance our weight like it was the very first time. Since it is not easy, it takes work every time and this is one reason I think a lot of us have difficulty with it. We don't like to do things over and over, especially if they are tough. But we must. Forgiveness is the most important task of our lives.

A common scenario

"I'm sorry."

"No, you are not."

"Yes, I am. I said I am sorry."

"You don't sound like you're sorry."

"What do you want me to do?"

"I want you to say you are sorry and mean it."

Whew! I think we have all lived that brief conversation. We must be willing to constantly improve our ability to ask for forgiveness and extend forgiveness in our daily lives, now more than ever.

Why is it so hard for us to ask for forgiveness and extend forgiveness? Why is it so hard for us to accept our humanity, recognizing that we will make significant mistakes that, unfortunately, will purposefully or not purposefully hurt other people? Why is it so difficult for us to accept the fact that some actions of others that hurt us are now in the past and we need to move on to improve our lives and the lives of others? I don't have the answers to these questions. Obviously, these very issues get to the root of human nature and interpersonal relationships. We live in an imperfect world, and we need to learn to accept the imperfections that we cannot change and change the imperfections we cannot accept.

We tend to make forgiveness conditional, yet God's forgiveness of our sins is unconditional. We are responsible for our actions and must accept the consequences of our actions. However, God does not extend forgiveness after some cooling off period. It is immediate. I must admit that I constantly struggle with these issues.

I have previously mentioned that forgiveness tends to be a developmental process, that our ability to forgive people at age ten is very different than our ability to forgive people at age thirty, fifty, or seventy. Hopefully, we learn over the course of our lifetime that forgiveness is essential for us to be able to move to the next developmental stages in life. Without the ability to forgive (not necessarily forget) we get stuck and cannot move on with the important work of our lives, to help others. Morrie Schwartz reminds us until we accept the responsibility for our mistakes and apologize, we cannot move on. We cannot get to the stage of forgiving others.

I wish we could teach more about forgiveness in schools. However, we must remember that the primary forgiveness skills are probably learned before the age of five years. Young children learn by the behavior of their parents. Children need to see their parents apologizing for their own mistakes and extending forgiveness to others who make mistakes. It is crucial that these lessons be learned early in life. We all need to learn how to do better.

A Difficult Example About Forgiveness

In an excellent book titled *The Language of God*, Francis Collins, a world-renowned scientist and geneticist, discusses his faith journey and his reconciliation of faith and science. He eloquently argues that faith in God and faith in science are harmonious and complement each other. Yet his faith journey provides a very challenging story that serves to emphasize the importance of forgiveness.

One night, one of his college-age daughters was brutally raped at knifepoint. The assailant was never caught. He relates the following after reflection about the incident:

> *We may never fully understand the reasons for these painful experiences, but we can begin to accept the idea [because of our faith in God] that there may be such reasons. In my case I can see, albeit dimly, that my daughter's rape was a challenge for me to try to learn the real meaning of forgiveness in a terribly wrenching circumstance. In complete honesty, I am still working on it...[It] was also an opportunity for me to recognize that I could not truly protect my daughters from all pain and suffering; I had to learn to entrust them to God's loving care, knowing that this provided not an immunization from evil, but a reassurance that their suffering would not be in vain.*

Dr. Collins's daughter experienced severe pain and suffering. Forgiveness in this set of circumstances must be one of the most difficult acts to perform, requiring time and significant internal energy. Yet faith in God and the life and lessons of Jesus Christ tell us that we must extend forgiveness (eventually) so we can use adversity to better our life and the lives of others.

THE TAKE-HOME MESSAGE

When it comes to personal and community activities, we need to remember what was in the past stays in the past, and we can always go forward in a positive way. Yes, mistakes can be rectified, responsibility can be accepted, and forgiveness practiced. We need to remember to forgive ourselves, forgive our neighbors, and move on. We can do it together on this life-long journey.

Chapter 51

Conflict Resolution

Two people are in conflict if they cannot agree. Sometimes the source of the conflict is a minor issue, sometimes a major issue. Sometimes the involved parties can have a rational discussion about the conflict, and sometimes they act irrational, being verbally or physically abusive.

The common thread is the inability to resolve conflict—inadequate conflict resolution. If we can't resolve conflicts, we tend to continue immature behavior like bullying. People who bully other people haven't learned how to deal with conflict. And those who are bullied and turn that anger into violence also haven't learned to deal with conflict.

The ability to resolve conflict in civilized society is probably not an innate ability. We have to be taught how to do it. We need to see positive role models in our parents, family members, employers, teachers, and fellow citizens. Even in the best of circumstances, conflicts are often difficult to resolve. If we have not had proper "training," we tend to overreact to conflict with bullying, yelling or hitting. When children see these exaggerated responses, they will understandably tend to mimic them as the way to deal with conflict. Adults (parents, family members, employers, teachers and governmental leaders) must set the proper positive example. If adults cannot do it, how do we expect children to do it?

Now, it's easy to say, "Don't overreact!" We all overreact to conflict at some time. When we do, we need to forgive ourselves (for our own mistakes) and we need to forgive others (for their mistakes). Without forgiveness, we can never learn conflict resolution. Without forgiveness, we are stuck in the past and cannot move forward.

A significant impediment to our personal and collective ability to accept and extend forgiveness is the inability to engage in rational discourse. What do I mean by rational discourse? One definition is "the ability to engage in a meaningful dialogue (listening to conflicting views and expressing one's own views) in a sensible fashion without demeaning the other individual(s) involved." Let me break it down to a few key elements.

- Meaningful—coming to the conversation with an open mind, not a closed mind;
- Dialogue—not a monologue;
- Listening—able to be quiet and truly hear what someone is saying;
- Sensible—calm and cool without hot-headed emotion; and
- Without demeaning—accepting our common humanity, not placing oneself above others

I don't see any of the above in current political exchanges; rather our current type of discourse is irrational and has been brewing for decades. We label people—Democrat vs. Republican, liberal vs. conservative, Tea Party member vs. socialist—and usually use the terms in a negative way. We call others idiots, criminals, and liars, often with no rational basis in fact. We assume that we know them by what we presume they stand for. We engage in conversations, but we are never really *engaged*. Our preconceived notions do not allow us to listen and process information. We often shout our views without really considering their impact on all concerned. We have taken away our ability to engage in rational discourse in the social arena. And we are the worse for it.

The progressive inability to engage in rational discourse severely hampers our ability to resolve conflicts and, more important, practice forgiveness. Our impressionable youth of today will view these heated exchanges and adopt this inappropriate behavior as the norm. They will not be able to understand the process of forgiveness. They will think that "ye who yells the loudest" is right and doesn't have to worry about the consequences.

THE TAKE-HOME MESSAGE

No one has a monopoly on wisdom. The most difficult task in our lifetime is learning the practice of forgiveness. If we cannot engage in rational discourse, we will never be able to forgive ourselves, to forgive others and to do it now. We will never make meaningful strides to improve ourselves and to improve our community.

Chapter 52

Communal Forgiveness

While learning how to practice personal forgiveness is difficult, it seems that social forgiveness is next to impossible in a society that always expects a solution via the legal system. Legal reparations are not always possible. Sometimes the most important step is for a group of people to accept their role in past problems, asking for forgiveness so society can move on, and deal with ongoing issues in a positive manner. We cannot accomplish effective change and work together until we acknowledge that we have been a part of a group that has harmed others in some way. We might agree that our group (social class, ethnic group, professional organization or the like) has committed a significant indiscretion toward others, but at the same time, we might argue that we as individuals did not do that, and that there should not be any guilt by association. I think that, with sincerity and humility, we need to honestly investigate the past to see if indiscretions have occurred. If so, we should work toward promoting the apology of our group. While we as individuals did not necessarily contribute to the wrong-doing, I think it is entirely appropriate to be a part of the reparative process. I don't know why we should do any less.

Let me use a recent "group" apology as an example. One of my professional organizations, the American Medical Association, just recently commissioned a panel of experts to review the history of race relations in medicine, especially regarding minority physicians. They concluded that the "principles (of the AMA)...compel physicians to treat each other, as well as their patients, without prejudice. In this regard the AMA failed, across the span of a century, to live up to the high standards that define the noble profession of medicine." So the AMA has issued an apology and a call to action "[1] to keep moving forward on a path toward eradication of prejudice and its harmful effects and [2] to achieve equality in society as a whole but especially in health care and public health."

Now is this just a hollow promise? I don't think so. Dr. Ronald Davis, past president of the AMA, recently discussed the importance of group apologies, explaining that they do the following:

- They formally acknowledge past wrongdoings, which will open up the door to healing fractured relationships;
- By acknowledging past wrongdoings, the group lays a path for tracking their actions now and in the future;
- Group apologies can help define a group's "moral compass" going forward; and
- Group apologies allow for current members of an organization (who likely bear little responsibility for past actions) to acknowledge that their group has been wrong in the past, making it clear that these current members would like to assist in the healing process going forward.

So the AMA has acknowledged that by its actions and inactions in the past it has contributed to the racial divide and potential disparities in health status and health care. Dr. Davis and the AMA want to ask for group forgiveness, reconciling current problems and moving forward in a positive fashion. This is not the AMA that I knew when I started my career, but I'm so thankful that the current AMA has changed. They are willing to face the reality of the past and make positive strides toward social equality in the present and future.

THE TAKE-HOME MESSAGE

Group apologies are extremely important. Sometimes that is the only way we can move forward in our society as we analyze our individual actions and our social actions. When we are wrong, we should extend forgiveness to ourselves and ask forgiveness from the harmed parties. Only then can we move forward to improve the lives of our fellow citizens.

Chapter 53

How to Move Forward

I recently finished a numbing book, *As We Forgive*. The book is numbing because it recounts multiple episodes of atrocities during the Rwandan genocide in 1994. Remember it is estimated that over 500,000 people were slaughtered over several months. The attackers were often their own neighbors. The survivors lost multiple loved ones and, more often than not, they were maimed themselves. Yet the survivors in this book were able to forgive their attackers. This process of forgiveness was an exceedingly painful one over an extended period of time, using pastors and counselors. The process of forgiveness required that the attackers be a part of this reconciliation process. This process of forgiveness was also a difficult one for the attackers (as those seeking forgiveness) because they had to work through all the issues associated with being involved in this genocide.

The book was numbing to me because I found myself asking – *would I be able to do the same thing* (extend forgiveness) *after enduring such horrific events?* I was numb when I truthfully answered *I don't know.* I don't know if I could reconcile with these assassins. Yet, I'm convinced that one of my main purposes in life is to learn forgiveness, practice reconciliation, and do it in the context of my own family, my community, and the society in which I live. That process means doing the simple things like avoiding unnecessary confrontations, listening, thinking twice before speaking, and recognizing that I'm not always right (to name a few). That process also means doing the difficult things, such as being able to engage in a positive way when it comes to issues that are often highly emotionally charged and seem to be irreconcilable. These latter issues—how to improve education or healthcare or the emotional well-being of our children, for instance—require an incredible amount of energy, yet it is crucial for us to recognize that forgiveness is essential to these processes if we want to make a positive difference.

What do forgiveness and public policy have to do with positive change? Actually, everything. We must recognize that we need to acknowledge past wrongs, listen to all sides, and begin to formulate policy for the common good. I think our lack of forgiveness is one of the primary problems when it comes to the inability of our politicians to work together for positive change. Everyone is so entrenched in their views or their own political persuasion that they cannot really listen and move forward.

The principles of forgiveness (extend forgiveness, accept forgiveness, and do it now) are lost in the shouting. The only way that we are able to improve our communities is to practice personal and social forgiveness in a calm manner. Debate and discussion are good, but calm resolution of problems is much better. If folks with serious problems can resolve their differences (such as the survivors of the Holocaust or the Rwandan genocide), why can't folks like us?

Revenge is Not the Answer

One of the subtitles in Dr. Fred Luskin's book, Forgive for Good, states that "holding a grudge is hazardous to your health." A key component of forgiveness then is the ability to recognize that we must direct our energies toward positive change after a serious offense or series of offenses. Dr. Luskin reminds us that "a life well lived is [our] best revenge. Instead of focusing on [our] wounded feelings, and thereby giving the person who caused [us] pain power over [us], learn to look for the love, beauty, and kindness around [us]." Holding a grudge does us no good except to take away the energy we need to improve ourselves and make things better.

If we already know all of the above, why do we still have such a hard time moving on? Because we have emotions and feelings that often get in the way. These emotions and feelings are normal, but need to be handled in a way to help us do positive things, not dwell on the problems and hurt of the past.

An Honest Answer

Even when we know we should do something, that doesn't mean we will do it. For example, smokers often know that smoking is bad for their health, but they just can't quit. We might know something in our minds that we should do, but we can't let our hearts do it. We are torn. This is the real paradox that makes forgiveness so difficult and makes the attainment of true forgiveness a lifetime task.

As I wrestled with these issues one night, I saw Lisa Beamer (widow of Todd Beamer, one of the many heroes on Flight 93 that crashed in Pennsylvania on 9/11/01) on television. The commentator noted that her husband's final act prior to attacking the hijackers was to recite the Lord's Prayer. Remember, one of the key passages in that prayer is about forgiveness – "forgive us our debts (or trespasses) as we forgive our debtors (or trespassers)." The commentator then asked Lisa the difficult question: could she forgive the terrorists? She paused, taken aback by the question, and then replied honestly that she really didn't think about that. But she was not going to let her thoughts and emotions toward those individuals keep her from moving forward and doing the right thing.

In other words, the whole issue of forgiveness for such a painful memory is still unresolved, but she would move on. She would continue to celebrate her husband's life by helping others to the best of her ability. She would raise their children to celebrate their father's love of life and his love for others. What a refreshingly honest answer. While she could not come to grips with forgiveness, she can put aside potentially very negative influences to continue to do what is important, helping others.

THE TAKE-HOME MESSAGE

While we often have a tough time dealing with forgiveness for painful issues (personal, business, social, or community), we can still move on, making sure we don't let our confusion cloud our actions. We must work together, taking communal responsibility, to improve the life of our community. Forgiveness will often take time and a lot of hard work.

Chapter 54

Forgiveness and Grace

Forgiveness continues to be the most difficult task in my life, and I suspect for others as well. Morrie Schwartz (author of *Tuesdays with Morrie*) reminds us of the three cardinal forgiveness principles mentioned earlier: 1) forgive yourself first, 2) forgive others, and 3) do it now. This order is important. We have to forgive ourselves first for harboring ill thoughts toward others, whether they have harmed us or not. The Lord's Prayer states the same order. In that prayer we ask for the forgiveness of our debts or trespasses, and then we are asked to forgive the debts or trespasses of others. We have to cleanse our soul first before we can truly open our hearts to extend forgiveness to others.

The final step in the process of forgiveness, then, is to do it now. Lingering unresolved conflicts do not benefit anyone and only serve to create larger rifts in relationships. Conflicts should be resolved as quickly and openly as possible. Morrie Schwartz, we remember, relates a very poignant example of unresolved conflict. He harbored ill will toward a friend due to an incident that in retrospect was just a misunderstanding. The friend died before he was able to reconcile this issue, and he sincerely regretted his inability to resolve this matter while his friend was still alive. We don't need to let similar situations happen to us.

Associated with forgiveness is the whole concept of grace in Christianity. The grace of God is "the free and unmerited favor or beneficence of God" and extended to us without any preconditions. If we accept grace for ourselves, we need to be able to extend grace as well. And that is why forgiveness is so tough. Doers of evil deeds need to be accountable to laws and their creator. We can make sure that they receive fair treatment under the laws of the land. We do not need to forget their deeds, but eventually we must extend forgiveness. Our job is to work toward extending grace as well as receiving it. The extension of grace to others in the same spirit in which it is given to us is *extremely* difficult. Our work is never done. That's why learning to practice forgiveness is a constant quest in our lives.

The Indulgence of Human Wrath

I hope we do not forget the root causes for many of our problems—the hatred and intolerance that are far too common in our society. I don't think enough children receive instruction on how to balance these negative images in order to work positively in our community. The key to this instruction is learning forgiveness.

Let me cite an historical perspective. Abraham Lincoln's future secretary of state, William Seward, lamented in the 1850s about the state of affairs in our country and, in particular, slavery: "They cannot see how much misery of human life is derived from the indulgence of wrath." Seward was referring to citizens who insisted on perpetuating the institution of slavery, but he could have been talking about anyone or any group of people who keep hatred in their hearts: individuals, groups of people, communities or society. Seward aptly noted that much misery is linked to hatred and intolerance. I think he would endorse the principles of forgiveness in a society expecting to move forward.

THE TAKE-HOME MESSAGE

Forgiveness and the grace of God are tied together. We cannot accept the grace of God without learning how to practice forgiveness. It is very hard, but it will make us better people and better citizens, allowing us to build better communities. Whether living in the 1850s with our country on the verge of civil war, or living at the present time, with intolerance ever present, we have to continually learn how to extend forgiveness for wrongs that have occurred and accept forgiveness for wrongs that we have committed.

Chapter 55

A Daily Process

I'm continually amazed (and, honestly, at times aggravated) at how difficult it is to exercise forgiveness properly. I've previously discussed the different developmental stages of forgiveness. At each of those stages, we have different levels of understanding. As children we are told how to say, "I'm sorry" and taught how to accept the apologies of others (usually our siblings). This stage involves acceptance of authority. The stages in adolescence and early adulthood are usually marked with an understanding of the need for forgiveness, but there is often difficulty in actually asking for and extending forgiveness. As we progress farther into adulthood, we should have learned some valuable lessons about forgiveness. That is, mistakes are made, feelings are hurt, and we learn how to accept these issues and move on. The stages of forgiveness reflect the stages of life as we mature and learn more ways to deal with less-than-perfect outcomes.

One of the most difficult aspects of forgiveness is the fact that we have to do it *all the time*. We'd like to think that once we recover from emotional trauma and extend forgiveness that we could move on. But more often than not, emotional issues resurface frequently and require a fresh round of forgiveness. We'd like to think that once we bury a hatchet we don't have to worry about those issues again. But experience tells us that we will have to revisit these issues again and be prepared to exhibit forgiveness again. We might think that we've already taken care of this or that, and then it happens again.

Why do things tend to recur? Why do we have to make the same mistakes and ask for forgiveness again? Because we're human! We all are capable of repeating our mistakes. And others are capable of committing the same mistakes that affect us. In response to those mistakes, we have to be able to exercise forgiveness, even for repeat offenses. Don't get me wrong. Other folks need to be held accountable for their actions, so repeat mistakes are not just accepted without question. But we need to be willing to extend forgiveness after satisfactory resolution of the issues.

A classic example of the latter is the usual problem adults have with adolescents. Adolescents frequently push the limits of acceptable behavior. When they go over the limit, parents will impose punishment and restrictions on future activities. When their children repeat their mistakes, parents will ask, "Why? Why did you do that? Haven't we talked about this before?" More often than not, certain problem behaviors have been discussed many times, but the repeat mistakes are just a part of adolescent behavior. As adults, our job is to make the adolescents accountable for their actions at the same time as we extend forgiveness, daily if necessary. We should never close the lines of communication.

THE TAKE-HOME MESSAGE

Personal and community improvement issues arise anew every day. It seems as though we invariably revisit these issues for improvement again and again, often without success. It's for this reason that we have to be prepared to roll up our sleeves daily and get to work. Everyday we need to forgive ourselves for our own inability to work well with others and forgive others for their mistakes. Never rest on yesterday's laurels. Today is a new day with new challenges.

Chapter 56

You Don't Have to Forget in Order to Forgive

Negative actions by others stir up emotions that make it difficult for us to deal with things calmly. We're upset, and sometimes it's hard to think straight. Plus, these emotions may have to be handled in the context of some major personal events (like a death in the family, family crisis, personal crisis, or divorce) or social events (like an unfavorable legal or political decision). These events can also complicate our ability to react calmly because we might feel that we have been personally wronged. We usually cannot separate our emotions from the events.

Some say that we need to forgive and forget when we are wronged. I heartily agree with the former (We need to forgive), but I disagree with the latter (We need to forget). If we are substantially harmed by some words or deeds, I think it's important to remember the circumstances so we will not repeat the same mistakes or find ourselves in the same unfortunate situation. *It is okay to remember.*

But if we truly forgive, we don't dwell on these past events.

Forgiveness does not demand that we forget bad things. Forgiveness does demand that we are sincere and humble in accepting apologies or extending apologies. And if we are sincere and humble, we will not dwell on past mistakes. We will use the lessons learned to improve our lives and the lives of others, but we will not try to belittle others under the guise of forgiveness.

THE TAKE-HOME MESSAGE

Life is a quest to learn about forgiveness. I think it is the hardest thing for us to learn and exercise toward others. We need to learn from bad things that happen in the past. But when we have extended or accepted forgiveness, it's time to move on with sincerity and humility. Only then can we help ourselves, our family, and our community.

Chapter 57

Children as Our Teachers

As infants, then children, and then adolescents, we have different abilities to cope with situations needing forgiveness. Our capabilities and the instruction from our parents lead to our ability to forgive others for mistakes and to ask forgiveness when we make mistakes. Sometimes people do not progress through the appropriate developmental stages and cannot learn to deal with mistakes or problems. They hold grudges, bully people, or seek violent means to resolve conflicts. If people don't learn how to exercise forgiveness or are not shown the right examples by adults, they don't progress and are stuck with immature ways to deal with problems. It is imperative that we view forgiveness as a learned skill that always needs improvement.

If we are going to learn forgiveness, whom can we look to as teachers? Our parents clearly are our primary teachers. Then our church family (including our pastor) and our school family (teachers and principals) should help us learn forgiveness and set the right examples. All of these instructors help us learn how to handle different situations—emotional situations, difficult situations, unfortunate situations, and situations that will test our abilities to exercise love for others. And when things don't go right, we'll have to ask for forgiveness and extend forgiveness based on our lessons learned.

But I think the best teachers for forgiveness are not mentioned above. I think the best teachers of forgiveness are our children. As a parent and as a pediatrician, I am constantly amazed and humbled by the comments and actions of children. If we really look and listen to our children, their comments and actions serve as a mirror for us. Their reactions to our words and behaviors show us how we are acting.

For example, children will more often than not forgive parents when the parents make mistakes. They will do this, usually with unspoken hugs, even when they may have been significantly hurt. This hurt might be physical or psychological. Parents might have yelled at them, told them to shut up or even hit them. While these acts are inexcusable, children seem to so easily forgive their parents. Why? Because they are vulnerable.

Consciously or unconsciously, children know that they need their parents, admittedly imperfect parents, to continue to be a source of support and hopefully comfort. The inherent vulnerability of children leads them to embrace their parents with a smile and an unspoken forgiveness even when adult logic would wonder why. I suspect that parents do not apologize often enough to their children when they make mistakes, but at least children extend forgiveness and want to move on. If children to not seek such comfort in an embrace, we need to ask some serious questions about our recent actions.

Maybe one of the reasons that adults do not accept vulnerability very well is that such a state reminds them of their childhood. They do not want to acknowledge that lack of control. Yet it is precisely the acknowledgement of vulnerability that is necessary for the whole process of forgiveness to move forward.

When we must discipline our children and extend forgiveness, we must do it in a loving way that emphasizes their importance. Conversely, if we are honest with ourselves, we often need to ask our children to forgive us for our words or actions. At the end of the day, we must analyze the comments and actions of our children to see if we are doing things right by seeing our reflections in our children and feeling good about it. If not, we should use these reflections to change our behavior in a positive way.

THE TAKE-HOME MESSAGE

If we hope to improve our community, forgiveness is one of the key elements. Forgiveness is tough. It's a constant process with lifelong learning, lifelong instruction, and lifelong introspection. Children can teach us a lot. Their actions speak to us if we will only look and listen.

Chapter 58

The Signs of Forgiveness

I'm a rabid sports fan and have to be careful not to spend too much time watching sports on TV. While I'm making confessions, I must also admit to being a movie addict. I love all types of movies: action, drama, comedy and any combination thereof. Though I often watch a movie to escape, I find that, more often than not, I will watch a movie, and then try to see how the characters or theme relate to my life.

One such movie is *Field of Dreams*. Set in rural Iowa, a farming family has a calling that leads them to build a baseball field. They do so, and experience a series of encounters that nobody else believes. At the end of the movie, the main character, Ray, is able to reconcile his differences with his deceased father. In one of the most poignant scenes I have ever seen, Ray realizes that this whole series of events that occurred throughout the movie were designed to help him come to grips with the issue of forgiveness and his father.

Ray and his father had a falling-out, and Ray vowed never to talk to his father again. His father died before they were able to reconcile with each other. At the end of the movie, Ray and his father come together and Ray appears to forgive his father for his stubbornness. But I think something much more important happens. Ray learns to forgive himself for his part in the disagreement that led to their bitter estrangement. Ray discovers that, to move on, he has to accept his role in the split (forgiving himself) before he is ready to understand and extend forgiveness to his father. One of the famous lines in the movie is, "If you build it, he will come." The "he" is not Shoeless Joe Jackson or even his father. The "he" is Ray himself. If he will accept this calling (building the ball field and the series of strange encounters to follow), he will finally reconcile with his father, forgiving himself and extending forgiveness toward his father. He "will come" full circle with these acts of reconciliation.

Now, some fans of the movie might disagree with my interpretation. This movie had an intensely personal message for me, so the interpretation is based on what the movie says to me.

As I learn to practice forgiveness, I learn that I must always initiate the process. What do I mean? Usually when we feel that an individual or group of individuals has committed a wrong against us, we feel hurt, anger, and bitterness. We can keep those feelings inside for a long period of time (and we often do), or we can move on after the initial shock and continue to improve our lives and the lives of those around us. By doing so, we do not let the wrong-doer alter or destroy our own lives. We have to recognize that we must make the first step (forgiving ourselves for our continued anger or bitterness) and then extend forgiveness. Only then can we continue to make a positive difference in the lives of our fellow citizens. I have to pay attention to the signs around me.

THE TAKE-HOME MESSAGE

Forgiveness is essential as we strive to improve ourselves and the lives of our fellow citizens. Let's pay attention to the signs (church, movies, and music, to name a few) that can provide the guideposts for us to recognize our current situation and make a positive change. This change (forgiving ourselves first) must occur before we can make a difference.

Chapter 59

Being Better Carpenters

"I don't think that I can ever forgive you."

"You don't mean it. You're not really sorry."

"When will you ever learn?"

Expressions such as these are repeated in households and workplaces everywhere every day of the week. We humans are social beings, and social beings interact. Interactions inevitably will lead to some conflict. I think our ability to resolve those conflicts defines our success in life, our ability to work with and for others.

At the heart of conflict resolution is the art of forgiveness. While conflict might be inevitable, it is how we deal with conflict that truly demonstrates our ability to make a positive contribution to our community. It has been said that the best carpenter is not necessarily the one who does the best work the first time, but the one who can best fix his mistakes. I think the same analogy holds for interpersonal and social relationships. Our ability to fix our individual mistakes and the mistakes of our community help us to move on in our lives. Recognizing that we make mistakes is the first part. When the mistakes occur, then we can work to correct the problems, asking for forgiveness for ourselves and extending forgiveness to others. Additional components to successful forgiveness are sincerity (truly meaning what you say and do) and humility (acknowledging that we are all equal in God's eyes).

I have previously discussed different stages of forgiveness, from childhood to adulthood. I now realize that that view is naïve. Even when we become adults, we still have several stages to go through in learning forgiveness. And adults often seem to have more difficulty with forgiveness, more than children or adolescents! Adults seem to think that words will sometimes suffice to express their forgiveness or their request for forgiveness, while words are just the promise of actions to come. Deeds demonstrate our true resolve, demonstrating how we care about our loved ones and others. Adults (myself included) take baby steps down the road to learning true forgiveness throughout our lives. The more steps we take with sincerity and humility and the more steps we take using deeds as the expression of our words and thoughts, the closer we are to really learning the meaning of forgiveness. I'm convinced that learning the meaning of forgiveness is our lifetime quest.

THE TAKE-HOME MESSAGE

Let's all be the best carpenters we can be, fixing our mistakes to the best of our ability. It is fitting that Jesus was a carpenter. He manifested the ultimate ability to forgive with sincerity and humility. We all have a lot to learn as we practice forgiveness.

I don't think our school was any different than any other high school in America

(Inscription from the wall of the Columbine Memorial)

Section 7
FINAL REMARKS

My intent in writing this book is to put forth a series of suggestions under the Five Steps to Community Improvement paradigm that will be of benefit to parents raising their children to be good citizens and contribute to the overall growth and improvement of our communities. We've discussed the Five Steps to Community Improvement: 1) learn to be the best parent possible, 2) get involved, 3) stay involved, 4) love for others, and 5) forgiveness. These steps are all necessary, in my view, if our children are to be the well rounded, contributing citizens that we all desire.

To that end, I originally proposed an illustration shown below to emphasize the inter-relationship of all of the Five Steps, placing each of the Five Steps at one of the points of a star. Because our sun provides light and energy for our lives and the stars light up the sky at night, I have always considered stars to be our figurative beacons of light. These beacons of light illuminate the paths that might lead us to helping others or to working for positive change in our own lives, hopefully both. These paths require work. We cannot just walk down the path and expect to find the answers. We have to actively engage in learning how to help others *and* improve our own lives. This is not a passive process, but an active one.

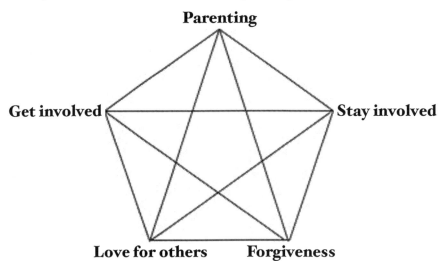

The "Five Steps Star" has five points, each point representing one of the steps needed to enhance positive change in our community. These points are the beacons of light, illuminating the paths to follow. Equally important, though, is the concept that these five points on the star are all interrelated and interdependent. These five paths are really just one path with five different but related components. Examples abound. One cannot seriously engage in community improvement by getting involved without practicing love for others and forgiveness. One cannot learn to be the best possible parent without getting involved in community affairs. One cannot profess love for others without practicing forgiveness. While our focus on learning one or more of these components might change from time to time, we need to remember to engage in all Five Steps consistently.

While we try to stay engaged at all levels, it is also important that we engage in what I call, the three Rs of adulthood. When I was a youngster, everyone talked about the three Rs of learning—reading, (w)riting, and (a)rithmetic, considered to be the basic tenets of learning. As we get into adulthood, we have to continue our learning efforts. The three Rs of adulthood have to do with our ability to adapt to change. They are review, renewal and recommitment.

- **Review**. One of the things we don't do very well in today's busy society is to take the time to review our lives. We need to review what has happened in our lives and what our responses have been. We need to review what we have done right, what we have done wrong, and how we can improve. We can't always change our circumstances or situation, but we can change our behavior. The purpose of reviewing, then, is to take stock of our lives, not dwelling on the past, but changing positively for the future. Without taking the time and energy to review our lives, we won't be able to improve our lives and the life of our community.
- **Renewal**. If we are honest with ourselves and review our lives faithfully, we will admit that it is time to renew our energies for things that make a difference in our lives, such as our spiritual

well being, our personal well being, our family's well being, and
our community's well being. Without this renewal of purpose and
spirit, we cannot truly make a difference.

- **Recommitment**. After reviewing our lives and renewing our
faith in ourselves and others, it is time to recommit our energies
to that purpose. Commitment means involvement with a sincerity
of purpose and with humility in action. We've all been committed
to various activities in the past. The way to take commitment to
a new level is to review life's experiences and to renew our sense
of purpose. We will now be equipped to truly recommit to activities that can make a difference in our lives and the life of our
community.

In early 2003, I had such an opportunity to review, renew, and recommit after serving for a year as the President of the Greenwood, SC Area
Chamber of Commerce. At the annual meeting, I was able to share some
remarks, titled Community is Family, based on that reflection:

*Last year at this meeting I commented that my father would not believe
that his son was now the president of the Chamber of Commerce, especially
after my long hair days in the late sixties, and it's fair to say the same about my
mother. Last month I buried my Mother, a single parent who did whatever it
took to provide for her sons and always set the right example. I'd like to think
that whatever positive attributes are attributed to me can be directly related
to my mother's influence in my life. However, because of her failing physical
and mental health, my Mother and I had far too many conflicts near the end
of her life. I had to make choices on her behalf that weren't popular, but had to
be made. I lost my "favorite son" status. But after her death (and this is the real
epiphany for me this year), I now know that she rests peacefully. I think she is
proud of her son and I can now see all the great things she did on my behalf during her life, unclouded by health and personality conflicts.*

*Why do I bring these intensely personal family issues to an annual meeting
of the Chamber of Commerce? Well, I'm a firm believer that if we're going to*

improve our community we have to treat each other as family. We might have difficult times, but in the long run, we are all in this together. Some of these difficult times might cloud our judgment, but we must remember that our community is our family. Often when we think in a business way we tend to lose sight of this big picture. We need to constantly remind ourselves that the real business of business is people. If we take care of people right, business will thrive, as well as our community. The Chamber of Commerce is focused on the business of business, people.

That's why I'm so proud of the work of the Greenwood Area Chamber of Commerce, the catalyst for so many community activities, such as park development, education, neighborhood, health and, cultural initiatives and workforce development, to name a few. And all of these activities complement our primary function, <u>business advocacy</u>. We exist to serve our members.

As you know, I started this series of articles after the shooting at Columbine High School in April 1999. I felt that it was important that each of us realize this could happen in Greenwood, and that we need to be taking positive steps to make sure that it doesn't.

The work of the Chamber of Commerce follows these same principles in its provision of services for you as members of the Chamber and for you as members of the community. Please be mindful of these steps the current year and beyond. Rest assured that the Chamber will continue working hard for our family, the Greenwood area community."

Another part of the three Rs process is the ability to change one's personal filters for how we interpret things. Writing the series of articles since 1999 forced me to consider reasonable suggestions for tangible ways to improve my community. At the same time, I noticed a change in the way I viewed and interpreted things. I seem to view movies, TV shows, sporting events, personal relationships, and social interactions through a different filter than before. I found a new sensitivity to issues, a sensitivity that allowed me to see opportunities that could make a difference. Unless we can see opportunities through a socially sensitive filter, we will not be moved to action. When we appreciate issues in our community with our revised filter, we learn to accept personal responsibility. Only then are we moved into action. We can now recognize that issues in the community will not change until we take personal ownership and become part of the solution by committing our personal resources.

So when we pause and reflect on our actions in our community, a new and improved filter (developed through continuous introspection) allows us to renew and recommit our energies toward community improvement. This is not easy or second nature, and requires significant work. Self-assessment shows that we need to change on a regular basis to really improve. Much as we need to change the filters on our home heating and cooling systems on a regular basis if they are to work efficiently, an honest self-assessment of our own actions should lead us to changing our own filters on a regular basis to improve how we interact with others and to changes in the community. Sometimes our filters get dusty and need to be swapped out with a clean filter. Only then can we move forward in a positive manner.

I would like to conclude with two dramatic and tragic events in the 21st century—September 11, 2001 and the Newtown shootings.

- September 11, 2001. I was in California at a medical meeting on that Tuesday in September 2001. Like the rest of the country, I was stunned. With two of my associates, we drove home as quickly as we could to be with our families. During the drive, I kept trying to understand what to do next. The message was eventually clear to me. *Now more than ever, we need to do whatever we can do to strengthen and improve our own community. I cannot think of a more respectful way to honor our fallen fellow Americans than to re-energize our efforts to realize the American dream for all of our citizens. Our fellow citizens died on American soil. We should honor them by doing everything in our power to improve our community, enhancing the American way of life.*
  Much as we honor the sacrifice of fallen soldiers, we should re-double our efforts to help our fellow citizens, paying homage to those that died on 9/11 and thereby, enhancing the American dream.

- Newtown, Connecticut. Like the entire nation, I was numb regarding the unspeakable events at Sandy Hook Elementary. After I heard the news on Friday, December 14, 2012, I really could not accomplish anything at work. The Columbine shootings in 1999 moved me to action, yet here we are again with another school shooting! What can we do? While I feel quite strongly about the need to enhance gun regulation and the need to provide better mental health care in our country, we must still continue to do whatever we can to improve the lives of our fellow citizens and our communities. *That is how we honor the fallen, by being the best citizens we can be.*

President Obama's remarks (below) at the Sandy Hook Interfaith Prayer Vigil on December 16, 2012 provide the appropriate conclusion to my concluding remarks for this book. It is my fervent hope that we continue to emphasize the importance of raising good citizens, always helping, not just *My Children's Children* but *all of our children's children.*

> *To all the families, first responders, to the community of Newtown, clergy, guests—Scripture tells us: "...do not lose heart. Though outwardly we are wasting away...inwardly we are being renewed day by day. For our light and momentary troubles are achieving for us an eternal glory that far outweighs them all. So we fix our eyes not on what is seen, but on what is unseen, since what is seen is temporary, but what is unseen is eternal. For we know that if the earthly tent we live in is destroyed, we have a building from God, an eternal house in heaven, not built by human hands."*
>
> *We gather here in memory of twenty beautiful children and six remarkable adults. They lost their lives in a school that could have been any school; in a quiet town full of good and decent people that could be any town in America.*
>
> *Here in Newtown, I come to offer the love and prayers of a nation. I am very mindful that mere words cannot match the depths of your sorrow, nor can they heal your wounded hearts. I can only hope it helps for you to know that you're not alone in your grief; that our world too has been torn apart; that all*

across this land of ours, we have wept with you, we've pulled our children tight. And you must know that whatever measure of comfort we can provide, we will provide; whatever portion of sadness that we can share with you to ease this heavy load, we will gladly bear it. Newtown—you are not alone.

As these difficult days have unfolded, you've also inspired us with stories of strength and resolve and sacrifice. We know that when danger arrived in the halls of Sandy Hook Elementary, the school's staff did not flinch, they did not hesitate. Dawn Hochsprung and Mary Sherlach, Vicki Soto, Lauren Rousseau, Rachel Davino and Anne Marie Murphy—they responded as we all hope we might respond in such terrifying circumstances—with courage and with love, giving their lives to protect the children in their care.

We know that there were other teachers who barricaded themselves inside classrooms, and kept steady through it all, and reassured their students by saying "Wait for the good guys, they're coming; Show me your smile."

And we know that good guys came. The first responders who raced to the scene, helping to guide those in harm's way to safety, and comfort those in need, holding at bay their own shock and trauma because they had a job to do, and others needed them more.

And then there were the scenes of the schoolchildren, helping one another, holding each other, dutifully following instructions in the way that young children sometimes do; one child even trying to encourage a grown-up by saying, "I know karate. So it's okay. I'll lead the way out."

As a community, you've inspired us, Newtown. In the face of indescribable violence, in the face of unconscionable evil, you've looked out for each other, and you've cared for one another, and you've loved one another. This is how Newtown will be remembered. And with time, and God's grace, that love will see you through.

But we, as a nation, we are left with some hard questions. Someone once described the joy and anxiety of parenthood as the equivalent of having your heart outside of your body all the time, walking around. With their very first cry, this most precious, vital part of ourselves—our child—is suddenly exposed to the world, to possible mishap or malice. And every parent knows there is nothing we will not do to shield our children from harm. And yet, we also know

*that with that child's very first step, and each step after that, they are separat-
ing from us, that we won't—that we can't always be there for them. They'll
suffer sickness and setbacks and broken hearts and disappointments. And we
learn that our most important job is to give them what they need to become self-
reliant and capable and resilient, ready to face the world without fear.*

*And we know we can't do this by ourselves. It comes as a shock at a certain
point where you realize, no matter how much you love these kids, you can't do it
by yourself. That this job of keeping our children safe, and teaching them well, is
something we can only do together, with the help of friends and neighbors, the help
of a community, and the help of a nation. And in that way, we come to realize that
we bear a responsibility for every child because we're counting on everybody else to
help look after ours; that we're all parents; that they're all our children.*

*This is our first task—caring for our children. It's our first job. If we don't
get that right, we don't get anything right. That's how, as a society, we will be
judged.*

*And by that measure, can we truly say, as a nation, that we are meeting
our obligations? Can we honestly say that we're doing enough to keep our children—all of them—safe from harm? Can we claim, as a nation, that we're all
together there, letting them know that they are loved, and teaching them to love
in return? Can we say that we're truly doing enough to give all the children of
this country the chance they deserve to live out their lives in happiness and with
purpose?*

*I've been reflecting on this the last few days, and if we're honest with our-
selves, the answer is no. We're not doing enough. And we will have to change.*

*Since I've been President, this is the fourth time we have come together to
comfort a grieving community torn apart by a mass shooting. The fourth time
we've hugged survivors. The fourth time we've consoled the families of victims.
And in between, there have been an endless series of deadly shootings across the
country, almost daily reports of victims, many of them children, in small towns
and big cities all across America—victims whose—much of the time, their only
fault was being in the wrong place at the wrong time.*

*We can't tolerate this anymore. These tragedies must end. And to end them,
we must change. We will be told that the causes of such violence are complex,*

and that is true. No single law—no set of laws can eliminate evil from the world, or prevent every senseless act of violence in our society.

But that can't be an excuse for inaction. Surely, we can do better than this. If there is even one step we can take to save another child, or another parent, or another town, from the grief that has visited Tucson, and Aurora, and Oak Creek, and Newtown, and communities from Columbine to Blacksburg before that—then surely we have an obligation to try.

In the coming weeks, I will use whatever power this office holds to engage my fellow citizens—from law enforcement to mental health professionals to parents and educators—in an effort aimed at preventing more tragedies like this. Because what choice do we have? We can't accept events like this as routine. Are we really prepared to say that we're powerless in the face of such carnage, that the politics are too hard? Are we prepared to say that such violence visited on our children year after year after year is somehow the price of our freedom?

All the world's religions—so many of them represented here today—start with a simple question: Why are we here? What gives our life meaning? What gives our acts purpose? We know our time on this Earth is fleeting. We know that we will each have our share of pleasure and pain; that even after we chase after some earthly goal, whether it's wealth or power or fame, or just simple comfort, we will, in some fashion, fall short of what we had hoped. We know that no matter how good our intentions, we will all stumble sometimes, in some way. We will make mistakes, we will experience hardships. And even when we're trying to do the right thing, we know that much of our time will be spent groping through the darkness, so often unable to discern God's heavenly plans.

There's only one thing we can be sure of, and that is the love that we have— for our children, for our families, for each other. The warmth of a small child's embrace—that is true. The memories we have of them, the joy that they bring, the wonder we see through their eyes, that fierce and boundless love we feel for them, a love that takes us out of ourselves, and binds us to something larger— we know that's what matters. We know we're always doing right when we're taking care of them, when we're teaching them well, when we're showing acts of kindness. We don't go wrong when we do that.

That's what we can be sure of. And that's what you, the people of Newtown, have reminded us. That's how you've inspired us. You remind us what matters. And that's what should drive us forward in everything we do, for as long as God sees fit to keep us on this Earth.

"Let the little children come to me," Jesus said, "and do not hinder them— for to such belongs the kingdom of heaven."

Charlotte. Daniel. Olivia. Josephine. Ana. Dylan. Madeleine. Catherine. Chase. Jesse. James. Grace. Emilie. Jack. Noah. Caroline. Jessica. Benjamin. Avielle. Allison.

God has called them all home. For those of us who remain, let us find the strength to carry on, and make our country worthy of their memory.

May God bless and keep those we've lost in His heavenly place. May He grace those we still have with His holy comfort. And may He bless and watch over this community, and the United States of America.

Acknowledgments

The support of countless people over the years has been a great source of encouragement to me. People who I didn't know approached me in the city of Greenwood to say they appreciated my articles in the newspaper and to please keep up the work. They often said the messages resonated with their situation and provided helpful advice. Since 1999 these words of encouragement have supplied significant energy for me to continue writing and to sustain the effort to prepare this book.

Specifically, I must acknowledge the folks below for their thoughtful review of numerous articles over the years and various drafts of the book. Their critical analyses of the material allowed the book to improve over the entire manuscript preparation process. Alphabetically, they are Fran Annese, Len Bornemann, Lorraine deJong, Susan DeVenny, Elaine Donoghue, Michelle Esquivel, Don Gordon, Mark Grimes, Glen Halva-Neubauer, Frank Holleman, Lucia Horowitz, Larry Jackson, Juan Johnson, Mark Kasper, Bob Lebel, Gay McHugh, Natalie Mikat-Stevens, John-Henry Pfifferling, Deb Richardson-Moore, Paul Spire, Juergen Spranger, Roger Stevenson, Carol Strickland, Beth Templeton, Tracy Trotter, and Suzan White. Martha Cook (Larkspur Consulting) did an outstanding job of copyediting. Beth Shaw of Stormcloud Studio, Munich, Germany designed the unique cover. The Interior Design staff of CreateSpace assisted with the interior layout.

A special thank you is in order to my editor, Patricia Horan, and to a dear friend of the Saul family, Scott Henderson. Patricia's thorough and remarkably helpful reviews helped direct the tenor of the book but always allowed me to have my own voice throughout. Scott provided the initial guidance for translating my writing into a manuscript with a unified message, and gently pushed me toward the necessary self-revelation that any author needs.

I am indebted to the following three gentlemen who provided endorsements for the book. Richard Riley is the former governor of South Carolina and Secretary of Education for 8 years under President Clinton. His soft-spoken nature belies his astute nature and his humanitarianism. I have had the pleasure to work with Jim Perrin, Professor of Pediatrics at Harvard Medical School, on several projects at the American Academy of Pediatrics and always found his insightful comments to be quite helpful. And Sam Katz, who was the Chairman of Pediatrics when I began my pediatric residency training at Duke University Medical Center, is one of those rare individuals a person meets in a lifetime who truly is a beacon of light to be followed. I am blessed to have known Sam as a student and mentor and now as a colleague and friend!

Finally, I thank the other Sauls in my life. My sons, Bradley and Ben, are the inspiration for my efforts to make a difference in the lives of my fellow citizens and my community. If I can have an influence in their lives as my mother did for me, then I will have succeeded and will leave with a smile on my face. I am so proud of their accomplishments and the fine young men they are. My wife, Jan, has been an incredible source of strength for me over the last 25 years. As I embarked on this Five Steps journey, she has supported me and encouraged me to express that inner voice and then to send the message out to others. Her help in this project is immeasurable as is my love for her. Thank you!

Bob Saul

About the author

Bob Saul was born in Chicago, IL and grew up in the Chicago area and later moved to Colorado. A graduate of Colorado College and the University of Colorado School of Medicine, he completed pediatric training at Duke University Medical Center and genetic training at the Greenwood Genetic Center. He is currently the Medical Director of General Pediatrics, Senior Medical Director of Pediatric Medicaid Practices, and Clinical Professor of Pediatrics at the Children's Hospital of Greenville Health System and the University of South Carolina School of Medicine – Greenville, Greenville, SC.

He has two grown children, Bradley and Ben, and has been married to his wife, Jan, for over 25 years. He is shown above at the Columbine Memorial in 2009, ten years after the shootings. Advocacy for children is his passion. This is his first book.

Notes

Chapter 1
- Leland Kaiser. www.kaiser.net/lee-kaiser

Chapter 3
- www.kidscount.org

Chapter 4
- pediatrics.aappublications.org/content/101/4/723.full
- Berlin LJ, Ispa JM, Fine MA, Malone PS, Brooks-Gunn J, Brady-Smith C, Ayoub C, Bai Y. Correlates and consequences of spanking and verbal punishment for low-income white, African American, and Mexican American toddlers. *Child Dev.* 2009 Sep-Oct;80(5):1403-20.

Chapter 5
- Nansel TR, Overpeck M, Pilla RS, Ruan WJ, Simons-Morton B, Scheidt P Bullying behaviors among US youth: prevalence and association with psychosocial adjustment. *JAMA.* 2001 Apr 25;285(16):2094-100.
- Arseneault L, Walsh E, Trzesniewski K, Newcombe R, Caspi A, Moffitt TE Bullying victimization uniquely contributes to adjustment problems in young children: a nationally representative cohort study. *Pediatrics.* 2006 Jul;118(1):130-8.

Chapter 6
- www.nytimes.com/2011/11/13/opinion/sunday/douthat-the-devil-and-joe-paterno.html?_r=0

Chapter 15
- pediatrics.aappublications.org/content/112/2/424.full

Chapter17
- Christakis DA, Zimmerman FJ, DiGiuseppe DL, McCarty CA Early television exposure and subsequent attentional problems in children. *Pediatrics.* 2004 Apr;113(4):708-13.
- Healy JM Early television exposure and subsequent attention problems in children. *Pediatrics.* 2004 Apr;113(4):917-8.

Chapter 19
- Garner AS, Shonkoff JP; Committee on Psychosocial Aspects of Child and Family Health; Committee on Early Childhood, Adoption, and Dependent Care; Section on Developmental and Behavioral Pediatrics. Early childhood adversity, toxic stress, and the role of the pediatrician: translating developmental science into lifelong health. *Pediatrics.* 2012 Jan;129(1):e224-31. doi: 10.1542/peds.2011-2662. Epub 2011 Dec 26.
- Shonkoff JP, Garner AS; Committee on Psychosocial Aspects of Child and Family Health; Committee on Early Childhood, Adoption, and Dependent Care; Section on Developmental and Behavioral Pediatrics. The lifelong effects of early childhood adversity and toxic stress. *Pediatrics.* 2012 Jan;129(1):e232-46. doi: 10.1542/peds.2011-2663. Epub 2011 Dec 26.

Chapter 22
- Putnam Robert D. Bowling Alone: The Collapse and Revival of American Community. New York: Simon & Schuster, 2000

Chapter 23
- Schacter-Shalomi, Zalman. From Age-ing to Sage-ing: A Profound New Vision of Growing Older. Time-Warner Books, 1997

Chapter 25
- My thanks to former President Carden Johnston, MD of the American Academy of Pediatrics, for providing a framework for the discussion.

Chapter 28
- Franzen, Jonathan. Liking is for Cowards. Go for What Hurts. New York Times, Sunday Opinion, May 29, 2011.

Chapter 31
- Albom, Mitch. Tuesdays with Morrie: An Old Man, a Young Man, and Life's Greatest Lesson. Broadway Books, 2002
- Albom, Mitch. The Five People You Meet in Heaven. Hyperion Books, 2006.

Chapter 37
- Kushner, Harold. The Lord Is My Shepherd: Healing Wisdom of the Twenty-third Psalm. Anchor Books, 2003.

Chapter 43
- Cournos, Francine. City of One, A Memoir. iUniverse, 2006.

Chapter 44
- My thanks to Pastor Ludwig Weaver of Westminster Presbyterian Church, Greenville, SC.

Chapter 50
- Collins, Francis. The Language of God: A Scientist Presents Evidence for Belief. Free Press, 2006.

Chapter 52
- www.ama-assn.org/ama/pub/news/speeches/ama-nma-past-present-future.page
- Information available in the July 16, 2008 issue of the *Journal of the American Medical Association* and at www.ama-assn.org/go/apology.

Chapter 53
- Larson, Catherine Claire. As We Forgive: Stories of Reconciliation from Rwanda. Zondervan, 2009
- Luskin, Frederic. Forgive for Good. Harper-Collins, 2010.

Made in the USA
Charleston, SC
02 May 2014